LA VIE RUSTIC

LA VIE RUSTIC

COOKING & LIVING IN THE FRENCH STYLE

GEORGEANNE BRENNAN

photography by SARA REMINGTON

weldonowen

to Ethel
& Oliver

CONTENTS

INTRODUCTION

ONCE UPON A TIME, I HAD THE PRIVILEGE OF LIVING AND WORKING IN RURAL PROVENCE, WHERE GROWING AND RAISING ONE'S OWN FOOD WAS A WAY OF LIFE. TO VARYING DEGREES, EVERYONE had a *basse-cour*, or "barnyard," that supplied eggs, the occasional chicken and rooster for the pot, guinea hens, rabbits, and sometimes ducks or goats as well. Everyone fatted a *cochon*, or "pig," to make the essential charcuterie, from salt-cured hams to pâtés for provisioning the home pantry.

A *potager*, the essential kitchen garden, planted and harvested throughout the year, supplied a family with vegetables, and a *verger*, or "orchard," was the source of fruits, nuts, and olives. Flowers were planted here and there because beauty should always be a part of life. Fruits and vegetables were harvested for the daily table. Some were preserved as well, with sugar or honey or in wine or vinegar, to use later in the year. For the most part, people took their wine grapes to the local wine-making cooperative, but kept a few bushels to make their own wine, too. Some households still baked bread with homegrown and home-milled grain; others fed their animals with hay, legumes, and grasses produced on their own land. The forest supplemented the bounty of the garden and orchard with mushrooms, truffles, wild asparagus, and dozens of tender wild greens. Thanks to the traditions of local hunting and fishing, wild boar, pheasant, and small birds were also part of the diet, as were trout and other fish from the rivers. Before supermarkets became common, a fishmonger from the coast had

a regular route through the backcountry of our region, stopping at outlying farms and hamlets. Sometimes people, especially those with friends on the coast, would make a sortie to the Mediterranean Sea and bring back sea urchins, mussels, sardines, or large fish to roast whole. The seasons dominated both the rhythm of activity and the food on the table.

Over the years, I learned how to cultivate a *potager*, sniff out the best spots for wild mushrooms, dress a lamb, make my own wine, and propagate fruit trees from cuttings. My neighbors taught me how to cure fresh pork in salt, make French-style pancetta (*roulade* or *ventrèche*), and cook wild birds over an open hearth.

EARLY YEARS IN PROVENCE

On a typical day in Provence, I might have used a traditional hand sickle to cut alfalfa for my neighbor's rabbits, cranked a wheel to draw enough well water to wash my family's laundry, including baby diapers, and helped prune wine grapes. Since we were raising goats for milk and to make cheese and pigs to sell as feeder pigs to be purchased young and fattened by others, a big part of my day was spent milking the goats, feeding the baby pigs, making cheese, and, of course, cooking.

My kitchen in those early years had just a two-burner gas cooktop and an ovenless, wood-burning stove that was primarily used for heat, though I sometimes used the small flat top to simmer a soup or stew. I didn't have an oven, but I became very adept and creative with my limited equipment. And since we picked and foraged much of our food ourselves, there was plenty of prep to be done: I had to wash the dirt off the radishes and lettuces, quadruple-wash the spinach and strawberries, and studiously rid the wild mushrooms of any clinging pine needles or oak leaves and of insidious creatures that may have burrowed inside. Sometimes I felt like I just didn't have the energy to do it all.

The cheese might refuse to curdle, a piglet would escape from its pen, and the sheepdog would follow the scent of a wild boar (or something), leaving the goats unguarded and scattered. Or perhaps I would just burn the vegetable stew. More than forty years later, I still have a scar on my knee from slipping on the icy ground in winter while trying to catch a goat. In the end, though, the cheese would succeed, the piglet would be captured, the dog would behave, and my next stew would be perfect.

Oddly enough, these days were among the happiest of my life, if also the most difficult. Even on bad days, providing sustenance for my family felt rewarding. The pleasure of rubbing wild thyme into a simmering pot of carrots, onions, sausage, and potatoes—peasant food—was thrilling to me. I learned the rhythm of nature and how it related to my daily life.

After two years and the birth of a second child, our son, we left Provence and moved back to California, where my husband and I became high school teachers. We kept our modest home in Provence and returned every summer, finding again, if for only a few months, that simple life. Without the responsibility of the animals and making a living from them, we were able to enjoy the life of summer visitors, but we were still considered part of the community. Neighbors became friends, and they shared their tables, invited us to weddings and holiday feasts, and told us stories of the two world wars that devastated their communities.

A divorce interrupted the thread of that early French life, but it has nevertheless continued with new friends and family that include a second husband of thirty years, two stepsons, and grandchildren, including a French son-in-law and half-French grandsons.

PROVENCE TODAY

When it comes to that part of Provence today, the traveling fishmonger is long gone, but the open markets continue. Village supermarkets have become more common, offering an astounding array of food, from fresh rabbit to organic cheeses. My neighbors still have big gardens and orchards, and I continue to learn something new about a sustainable life whenever I visit. I admit, however, that I am grateful for the hot and cold running water and my washing machine. I don't have room for a dishwasher or a clothes dryer, but if I did, I would install them. I now have a four-burner gas stove and an electric oven outfitted with a rotisserie. Even though the oven is twenty-five years old, it serves me well.

Along the way I've learned such wide-ranging things as the traditional thirteen desserts of a Provençal Christmas (page 126), the history of snail farms (page 197), how to clean and eat a sea urchin (page 275), and how some olive mills still use heavy stone wheels to crush the fruit to oil.

Little did I know it at the time, but my first years in France gave me the foundation for my life's work as an entrepreneur and food writer and changed me forever. The more I learned, the more I began to realize not only how delicious these foods were, but how this relationship between land and table is more than just sustenance—it is the warp and woof of French life, no matter how humble or grand. The tapestry has become more fragile and frayed in urban areas, true, but in the small villages and rural regions that form the landscape of so much of France, the matrix of barnyard, orchard, garden, and the wilds of land and water is not an artifact of a bygone era or a show put on for tourists. It remains the basis of daily life, if not in practice, at least in spirit.

People from the cities still head out to the country on the weekends, to visit family and friends, to have a long lunch, and to bring home whatever is locally grown or produced. The sea draws them with early-morning fish markets and sea urchin collecting. In fall, cars line the roadsides helter-skelter, temporarily abandoned by their owners who've gone in search of mushrooms.

This way of thinking, cooking, and eating made sense to me all those years ago. It still makes sense to me now, which has led me to create a new company and product line, La Vie Rustic—Sustainable Living in the French Style. I've created and sourced— and continue to do so—a wide variety of products that encompass the breadth of the French way of life. My intent is to offer anyone, anywhere the opportunity and access to experience at least a small part of the joy of that French style, in which garden and orchard, barnyard, field, and forest are all linked and come together in the kitchen over food and around the table.

It's not my first experience in the specialty goods market. In the early 1980s, I was a cofounder of Le Marché Seeds, a pioneering specialty and heirloom vegetable seed company. I know firsthand the sense of continuity it gives a gardener, even the first-timer, to plant seeds whose provenance date back to the nineteenth-century market gardens of France. And so heirloom seeds are among La Vie Rustic's products, along with bouquets of fresh sweet bay laurel from my small farm, young fig trees I've grown from cuttings that have their origin in Algeria, charcuterie sets, pasture mixes for chickens,

herb and specialty salt collections, and handmade ceramics reminiscent of those you find in Provence.

La Vie Rustic: Cooking & Living in the French Style is, like the company, rooted firmly in French tradition, which is imminently useful in today's complex, global world. Just thinking about food from the perspective of sowing, planting, and harvesting with the rhythms of the seasons conjures a little bit of France no matter where you live.

HOW TO USE THIS BOOK

The book is divided into five chapters, The Potager, The Orchard, The Barnyard, The Forest & Field, and The Water. In the recipes, as in life, there are connections and areas of overlap, which will become apparent as you read and cook from them. Each chapter includes a range of appetizers, soups, salads, main dishes, side dishes, and, when appropriate, desserts.

And each chapter includes some do-it-your-self projects, such as making stove-top goat cheese, fruit-infused wine, or pickled mush-rooms, giving you an opportunity for French-style rusticity no matter where you live.

Throughout the book, chapter by chapter, there are sidebars in which I share some of my favorite bits of French history, contemporary French manners, gardening and growing, animal husbandry, and culinary skills.

Finally, I've included one or more very simple narratives that will encourage you to trust your instincts and cook without a recipe—part of the French way of thinking about food, kitchen, and the table.

CHAPTER ONE

THE POTAGER

THE POTAGER

YEAR-ROUND VEGETABLES

I DISCOVERED THE *POTAGER*, OR "KITCHEN GARDEN," WHEN WE FIRST MOVED TO PROVENCE. EVERYONE IN THAT PART OF FRANCE HAD A GARDEN, AND EVERY DAY, someone from the household would go out to gather the foundation of the day's meals. The vegetables changed with the seasons, and seeds and seedlings were planted all year long, ensuring a continuous flow of food.

The importance of a *potager* in the scheme of French country life cannot be overestimated. The deed to my house in Provence specifies, among the several parcels of land, barns, and outbuildings, *un potager*. The designated piece of land for this garden is adjacent to a field and next to a well, a hefty distance from the main building. This is not unusual, however. In the grand scheme of French rural life, even as property was divided in inheritances, each dwelling had to have what was needed for a sustainable life. In my case, this included a plot for a vegetable garden, a bit of land for trees and crops, space to keep animals, a share of the threshing ground, and a source of water.

My *potager* is now planted and kept thriving by my neighbor, and whenever I am there, I am welcome to pick whatever I want. All year long, there is something flavorful to eat to be found in the garden.

Ever since my initiation into the tradition of the *potager*, it has been one of the most rewarding aspects of my life. When my first husband and I moved to a suburb in Northern California after returning from France, we established a *potager* in our front yard. After digging up half the lawn, we planted peas, radishes, carrots, and lettuces in early spring, followed by squashes, eggplants, and peppers for summer. We couldn't find seeds for fava beans, so a French friend mailed some to us. We harvested from the garden all spring and summer long, and our table was never bereft of fresh vegetables. Our two small children readily ate the grilled eggplant and zucchini we cooked, and they were happy to eat the fresh radishes and

carrots directly from the garden. As fall's cooler weather approached, we planted cool-weather crops like broccoli and cauliflower and made salads throughout the fall and winter.

My garden now is larger than that first one, at more than 4,000 square feet (370 sq m), and it feeds us year-round and provides us with enough vegetables to share with friends and neighbors. I've expanded my culinary loot with plantings of celery root, potatoes, alliums of all kinds, favas (of course), asparagus, kale, and collards. And I still cultivate the staples of radishes, beans, peppers, tomatoes, lettuces, chicories, and eggplants.

Today, all of my children have their own vegetable gardens, from a backyard in San Francisco's Mission District to raised beds in a Portland, Oregon, side yard, and they cook from them on a daily basis, bringing my grandchildren along to help with the harvest.

GREEN HERB SALAD with
FAVA LEAVES & MANDARINS

Fava beans are a must-have in French potagers because they come early in the season and are a welcome change after winter's hardy vegetables. I know that is how I feel about favas, and I make sure to plant rows of them in my garden every year. The leaves, which have the same meaty, green flavor as the beans, can be used in salads for the earliest taste of spring. If you can't find fava leaves at your farmers' market, you could substitute pea shoots or tender spring lettuce.

In a salad bowl, whisk together the oil, vinegar, shallot, salt, and pepper. Add the fava leaves, parsley, chervil, tarragon, and half of the mandarins and toss gently to coat. Scoop a mound onto each of 4 salad plates and top with the remaining mandarins. Serve at once.

SERVES 4

3 Tbsp extra-virgin olive oil

1 Tbsp Champagne vinegar

1 tsp minced shallot

¼ tsp sea salt

¼ tsp freshly ground pepper

2 cups (2½ oz/75 g) young, tender fava leaves

1 cup (1 oz/ 30 g) fresh flat-leaf parsley leaves

½ cup (½ oz/15 g) fresh chervil leaves

2 Tbsp fresh tarragon leaves

3 mandarin oranges, peeled, sectioned, seeded, and halved crosswise

THE SIMPLEST SALAD

Nothing is easier to make than a fresh salad. I like to mix the dressing—usually vinaigrette for me—directly in the salad bowl. That way, the leaves will be equally well dressed when I toss them, and I'll have one less bowl to wash. For the dressing, I use 2–3 parts extra-virgin olive oil to 1 part acid, such as red, white, Champagne, or any other kind of vinegar; fresh lemon juice; or other citrus juice. Season with sea salt and freshly ground pepper and mix well. Check to make sure your lettuce leaves are dry, so the dressing won't get watered down. Tear your clean, dry lettuce leaves—small ones can be left whole—toss them with the dressing, and voilà! A simple salad can be served on its own or used as a base for other ingredients, such as fresh herbs, herb blossoms, cheese, vegetables, fresh fruits, cured meats, croutons, or even grilled meat, fowl, or fish.

CHARRED ARTICHOKES with FRESH HERB DIPPING SAUCE

Artichokes vary in size and type. In Brittany, the large, green globe artichokes are the standard, but in the south of France, the smaller, pointed types predominate, and they may be green or purple. I have both kinds in my garden, and for this dish, any variety of artichoke can be used, large or small. Marinating the artichokes before grilling deeply enhances their flavor.

To make the sauce, in a bowl, stir together the yogurt, mayonnaise, parsley, tarragon, chives, lemon juice, salt, and pepper. Taste and adjust the seasoning. Cover and refrigerate until ready to use.

To prepare the artichokes, cut off the stem of each artichoke so that it's flush with the base, then cut off the top one-third (the prickly leaf ends) of each artichoke. Pour water into the bottom of a steamer pot to a depth of about 3 inches (7.5 cm), put the rack in place, and bring the water to a boil over high heat. Place the artichokes, stem end up, on the rack, reduce the heat to medium, cover, and steam until the base of an artichoke offers little resistance when pierced with the tines of a fork, 20–30 minutes. The timing depends on the size and maturity of the artichokes.

Remove the artichokes from the steamer and set aside to cool. When cool enough to handle, cut the artichokes in half lengthwise with a sharp knife. Using a spoon, scoop out the center leaves from each artichoke, removing the thistles and any furry bits.

In a bowl large enough to hold all of the artichokes, combine the parsley, garlic, oil, lemon juice, salt, and pepper. Turn several times to coat well. Let marinate at room temperature for at least 20 minutes, or up to 4 hours.

Prepare a charcoal or wood fire in a grill or preheat a gas grill. When the grill is hot, place the artichokes cut side up and grill until charred, turning them with tongs so all of the outer leaves get charred, about 3 minutes. Flip and grill the cut side until charred, about 3 minutes longer. Transfer to a platter and let cool to room temperature. Serve with the dipping sauce.

SERVES 8 AS AN APPETIZER OR SIDE DISH

for the sauce

1 cup (8 oz/250 g) plain nonfat yogurt

1 cup (8 fl oz/250 ml) mayonnaise

¼ cup (⅓ oz/10 g) minced fresh flat-leaf parsley

1 Tbsp minced fresh tarragon

1 Tbsp minced fresh chives

1 tsp fresh lemon juice

¼ tsp sea salt

¼ tsp freshly ground pepper

for the artichokes

4–6 artichokes, depending on size

½ cup (¾ oz/20 g) minced fresh flat-leaf parsley (from about 1 bunch)

2 cloves garlic, minced

2–3 Tbsp extra-virgin olive oil

1 tsp fresh lemon juice

½ tsp sea salt

½ tsp freshly ground pepper

PAN-ROASTED SPRING ONIONS

In early spring, onion plants begin to bulb and the bright green stalks are tender, unlike mature onions, whose stalks become fibrous and eventually dry. These so-called spring onions can be used in their entirety and prepared in the simplest of ways, either on the grill or in the oven as they are here. Serve these pan-roasted alliums as a side dish to accompany pork, chicken, or other meats, or chop them to garnish polenta or sandwiches. They also add a depth of flavor to soups and stews.

Preheat the oven to 350°F (180°C).

Trim the stringy root ends from the onions, but do not cut into the bases, which help hold the onions together as they roast. Trim the dark green tips from the stalks. Cut each onion in half lengthwise and place in a roasting pan. Pour the oil over the onions and gently turn them to coat. Season with salt and pepper, add the thyme, and gently turn again.

Roast the onions, turning once, until caramelized and slightly charred, 35–45 minutes.

Serve hot or at room temperature.

SERVES 4–6

6 spring onions, with golf ball–size bulbs, with stems

3 Tbsp extra-virgin olive oil

Coarse sea salt and freshly ground pepper

6 fresh thyme sprigs

A PICKLE PLATTER

*At the start of a French meal, there is always a place on the table for pickles,
often to accompany charcuterie such as rillettes (page 151), pâtés (page 150), or
cured meats. The sharpness of the pickles serves as a counterpoint to the richness
of the meats, making for a pleasant balance. Cornichons, the tiny cucumbers
pickled with vinegar and tarragon, are the most common, but a fine selection
of refrigerator pickles can be made using spring's delicate vegetables —and
they keep for several months. These are all young, early crop baby vegetables
that you can find at a farmers' market, if not in your own garden.*

Wash three 1-pt (16–fl oz/500-ml) canning jars and their lids
in hot, soapy water, dry well, and set aside. Cut the carrots in
half on the diagonal, then cut lengthwise into ¼-inch (6-mm)
slices. Trim the fennel bulbs, leaving ¼–½ inch (6–12 mm) of
their fronds intact, then halve them lengthwise. Trim the turnips,
leaving ½ inch (12 mm) of their greens intact, then halve or
quarter them lengthwise.

Pack the carrots and dill into 1 of the jars. Pack the fennel
and fennel seeds into a second jar. Pack the turnips and
mustard seeds into the third jar. Add ¼ teaspoon of the
peppercorns to each jar.

In a large nonreactive pan, bring 8 cups (64 fl oz/2 l)
water, the vinegar, and salt to a boil over medium-high
heat, stirring to dissolve the salt.

Ladle the hot brine into the jars, filling each to within
½ inch (12 mm) of the rim. Seal each jar tightly with a lid,
then turn the lid back a quarter turn to allow for expansion.
Set the sealed jars on a kitchen towel to cool overnight.

The next day, tighten the lids. Store the pickles in the
refrigerator for up to 6 months.

MAKES 3 PINTS
(48 FL OZ/1.5 L)

1 lb (500 g) young
carrots, about 4 inches
(10 cm) long, with tops

24 baby fennel bulbs,
each 1–2 inches
(2.5–5 cm) long

24 baby turnips, about
the size of large marbles,
with tops

2–3 fresh dill sprigs

1 tsp fennel seeds

1 tsp mustard seeds

¾ tsp black peppercorns

4 cups (32 fl oz/1 l)
cider vinegar

¾ cup (7 oz/220 g)
pickling salt or sea salt

CLASSIC FRENCH PEAS
& BUTTER LETTUCE

There are few greater springtime treats than fresh peas. On two occasions, I've been invited into a field of peas to pick my fill. What an amazing time, to come home with two large basketfuls brimming with fresh peas. I didn't mind shelling them at all, and in both instances, we ate peas for three days straight without tiring of them.

In this basic recipe, the peas literally cook in the natural moisture of the lettuce and that little bit of butter that is added. I like to serve these with something simple, like a roast chicken or grilled meat, that allows the peas to be the star of the plate.

Coarsely chop the lettuce and finely chop the white parts of the green onions and half of the green parts, discarding the rest.

In a large sauté pan, melt the butter over medium-high heat. When it foams, add the lettuce and green onions and toss to coat. Add 1 tablespoon of the broth, reduce the heat to low, cover, and cook until the lettuce is thoroughly wilted, about 5 minutes.

Add the peas, stir to combine, re-cover the pan, and cook until the peas are tender, 3–5 minutes if young, slightly longer if more mature. Add 1 more tablespoon broth, if needed, during the last few minutes of cooking time. Stir in the salt and pepper, then taste and adjust the seasoning.

Serve at once.

SERVES 4

1 large head butter lettuce

2 bunches green onions

1 Tbsp unsalted butter

1–2 Tbsp chicken broth, homemade (page 166) or purchased

3 lb (1.5 kg) English peas in the pod, shelled

½ tsp sea salt

¼ tsp freshly ground pepper

TREE PRUNINGS FOR VINING VEGETABLES

Traveling through France, looking at gardens, I was struck by the peas and beans that twisted in and around pruned tree branches, stuck into the ground in either teepee shapes or double rows. They looked much prettier and were infinitely more practical than the metal stakes or galvanized wire trellises or cages that I was used to seeing in gardening catalogs and nursery centers. Using prunings from the orchard for vegetables in the garden seems so logical and sustainable. When the prunings have served their purpose, they are cut into shorter lengths and used for kindling or chopped and composted.

GREEN GARLIC & NEW POTATO SOUP

Green garlic appears during a small window in spring when the garlic bulb is beginning to form but is still tender. The garlic's pungent oils are developing as well, so the flavor of green garlic is milder than when it is mature. The gentle taste of the young garlic infuses this simple yet elegant cream soup.

Trim the stringy root ends and all but ½ inch (12 mm) of the stalks from the bulbs of green garlic. Peel away the outer layer from the bulbs and chop the bulbs.

In a saucepan, melt the butter over medium-high heat. When it foams, add the garlic and shallot and cook, stirring, until soft, about 3 minutes. Add the broth and bring to a boil, then reduce the heat to low and simmer until the broth is infused and the garlic is exceedingly soft, about 4 minutes.

Place a chinois or fine-mesh sieve over a clean saucepan and strain the garlic broth, pressing on the garlic and shallot with the back of a spoon to extract the maximum flavor. Discard the solids. Return the strained garlic broth to the saucepan, add the potatoes, and bring to a boil over medium-high heat. Reduce the heat to medium and cook until the potatoes are soft and easily pierced with the tines of a fork, about 20 minutes.

Using an immersion or upright blender, purée the soup until smooth. Over a clean saucepan, strain once again through a chinois or fine-mesh sieve, gently pressing against any remaining solids.

Place the saucepan over medium heat and bring the purée to just below a simmer. Stir in the salt and pepper, followed by the crème fraîche. Taste and adjust the seasoning. Ladle the soup into bowls and serve at once.

SERVES 4

8 stalks green garlic

2 Tbsp unsalted butter

2 Tbsp minced shallot

4 cups (32 fl oz/1 l) chicken broth, homemade (page 166) or purchased

3 new potatoes, peeled and cut into 1-inch (2.5-cm) cubes

¼ tsp sea salt

¼ tsp freshly ground white pepper (or black, if you don't mind the specks)

1 Tbsp crème fraîche

SIMPLE SOUPS

A vegetable soup can be made in the briefest of time. Begin
by sautéing chopped onion in a little fat—I use either butter or
extra-virgin olive oil, or sometimes lard—to provide a base flavor.
Next, add chopped vegetables, such as carrots, celery, broccoli,
or cauliflower in spring and winter, or peppers, eggplants, beans,
or squashes in summer and fall. Sauté them briefly, then add a
broth of your choice, sea salt, freshly ground pepper, and, if you
want extra thickening, some cubed potatoes and simmer until
the vegetables are tender, 15–30 minutes. The final steps are
to purée the soup, making it smooth or a little chunky, as you
like, and then to reheat it, taste, and adjust the seasoning. It can
be served as is or dressed up with a garnish, such as croutons,
crispy bits of lardons, a fresh herb, sour cream, or crème fraîche.

FENNEL & CHICKEN BRAISED with LEMON

*Fennel is good both raw and cooked. Cooking transforms its distinct licorice
flavor into an almost-sweet back note. From the garden, I like to use very
young fennel for pickles (page 19) and the larger, more robust bulbs for
gratins and in braised dishes like this one. Since I have Meyer lemon trees
at my house in California, I use them here, though any variety will work.*

Trim the stalks from the fennel, reserving the lacy tips of the
fronds for garnish. Cut the fennel bulb lengthwise into ¼-inch
(6-mm) slices—the slices will look like hands. Cut the fennel
"hands" lengthwise into ½-inch (12-mm) slices. Set aside.

Put the lemons in a bowl and sprinkle with the salt. Add the
chicken, garlic, oregano, and pepper and turn to coat. Let
stand for about 30 minutes for the flavors to infuse the chicken.

In a heavy-bottomed saucepan or Dutch oven, heat 1 tablespoon
of the oil over medium-high heat. When it is hot, add the chicken
thighs, reserving the lemon pieces, garlic, and oregano, and cook,
turning several times, until lightly browned, about 10 minutes.
Transfer the chicken to a plate or platter.

Pour the remaining 1 tablespoon oil into the hot pan and add
the fennel. Reduce the heat to medium and sauté, stirring, until
nearly translucent, 8–10 minutes. Stir in the lemons, garlic,
and oregano, turning a few times. Add the wine and ½ cup
(4 fl oz/125 ml) water and deglaze the pan by scraping up any
bits that cling to the bottom. Return the chicken to the pan,
cover, reduce the heat to low, and cook until the chicken is
tender and the fennel can be cut with a spoon, about 45 minutes.

While the chicken is cooking, mince enough of the fennel
fronds to measure 2 tablespoons. Combine the chopped
fronds with the lemon zest.

Transfer the chicken mixture to a platter and garnish with
the lemon-fennel mixture and the olives. Serve at once.

SERVES 4

1 large or 2 medium
fennel bulbs, with
stalks and fronds

2 lemons, preferably
Meyer, halved then
cut into 3 pieces

1 tsp sea salt

6 chicken thighs,
with or without skin

2 cloves garlic, minced

1 tsp dried oregano

½ tsp freshly
ground pepper

2 Tbsp extra-virgin
olive oil

½ cup (4 fl oz/125 ml)
dry white wine

2 Tbsp grated lemon zest

¼ cup (1¼ oz/35 g)
green olives, pitted

SPRING VEGETABLES with LAMB RIBLETS

Lamb and spring vegetables are a mainstay of French home cooking, where they are often combined in a ragout to which cream is added. The small seasonal vegetables — turnips the size of walnuts, carrots that are slim and not too long, delicate potatoes, sweet peas — are called primeurs *in French, and here I roast all but the peas and then serve them along with lamb riblets in a deconstructed version of the French classic that is crisp rather than creamy. You may need to special order the lamb ribs, which come in slabs of varying sizes and are usually labeled "riblets" or "lamb breast."*

Preheat the oven to 375°F (190°C). Place racks in the upper and lower thirds of the oven. The lamb and vegetables will be roasted at the same time but on different baking sheets.

Rub the lamb racks with half each of the salt and pepper and the herbes de Provence and place on a rimmed baking sheet on the upper rack of the oven. Roast, turning twice, until the meat between the ribs is easily pierced with the tip of a knife, 40–50 minutes.

Place the carrots and turnips on a separate rimmed baking sheet and toss with 2½ teaspoons of the oil and the remaining salt and pepper. Place on the lower rack of the oven and roast, turning several times, until slightly caramelized and easily pierced with the tip of a knife, 30–40 minutes.

Put the potatoes in a saucepan, add water to cover by 2 inches (5 cm), and bring to a boil over medium-high heat. Reduce the heat to low and simmer until soft and easily pierced with the tines of a fork, 15–20 minutes. Drain the potatoes, then add to the carrots and turnips, along with the remaining ½ teaspoon oil, during the last 10 minutes of roasting.

In a saucepan, bring 1½ cups (12 fl oz/375 ml) water to a boil over medium-high heat. Add the peas, reduce the heat to medium, and cook just until the peas are tender, about 5 minutes. Drain and return to the pan to keep warm.

Place 1 lamb rack on each of 4 warmed dinner plates. Divide the roasted vegetables equally among the plates alongside the lamb, then top with the peas, scattering them evenly. Serve at once.

SERVES 4

2 lb (1 kg) lamb riblets, cut into 4 racks

2 tsp sea salt

½ tsp freshly ground pepper

½ tsp herbes de Provence

2 bunches young carrots (about 15), tops trimmed to ¼ inch (6 mm) and carrots halved lengthwise

2 bunches golf ball–size turnips, tops trimmed to ¼ inch (6 mm) and turnips halved lengthwise

3 tsp extra-virgin olive oil

1½ lb (750 g) small new potatoes

1 lb (500 g) English peas in the pod, shelled

STRAWBERRY MOUSSE

Strawberries are often planted along the borders of potagers. *They are the first fruits to appear in spring and are frequently served marinated in red wine and sugar. For a fancier yet still easy dessert, try this strawberry mousse.*

Using a blender, purée the strawberries until smooth. Strain the purée through a chinois or fine-mesh sieve if you don't want seeds in the mousse. Transfer the purée to a large bowl and stir in the sugar.

In a small saucepan, bring ¼ cup (2 fl oz/60 ml) water to a boil over high heat. Remove from the heat, sprinkle the gelatin over the top, and let stand until dissolved, about 5 minutes.

Whisk the dissolved gelatin into the strawberry purée. Let cool to room temperature.

In a bowl, whip the cream to soft peaks. Fold the whipped cream into the purée. Spoon the mousse into 6–8 decorative dessert glasses or bowls and refrigerate for at least 2 hours, or up to 2 days.

Serve chilled, garnished with the strawberry slices.

SERVES 6-8

1 pt (8 oz/250 g) strawberries, stemmed and cored, reserving 4 strawberries, sliced, for garnish

⅓ cup (3 oz/90 g) sugar

1 Tbsp (1 package) unflavored gelatin

1 cup (8 fl oz/250 ml) heavy cream

A LETTUCE PRIMER

Lettuce comes in many colors, from deep magenta red to darkest green. There are several types of lettuces, in a wide range of sizes, shapes, and colors, but they all fall into one of these four main categories.

BATAVIAN OR CRISPHEAD

Batavian lettuces are somewhat old-fashioned, with a semitight head and looser outer leaves. They are the precursor to the crisphead or iceberg types so commonly seen today, with their exceedingly tight heads and lots of wrapper leaves, which are generally discarded before the lettuces are sent to market. One of my very favorite lettuces, the heirloom Reine des Glaces, which I always grow in my garden, belongs to this category. It has a crunchy texture, beautiful lace-edged leaves, and a flavor akin to iceberg but more pronounced. To dress it, I like to make a basic vinaigrette, then add a blue cheese such as *fourme d'Ambert* or Gorgonzola to both the dressing and the salad. The crisp leaves stand up to the sturdy dressing.

BUTTERHEAD

Butterhead lettuce forms small to medium heads comprised of loosely folding, fine-textured leaves. The leaves are very smooth and delicate, making these lettuces a favorite in France for the classic mustard vinaigrette that thickly coats the leaves. Merveille des Quatre Saisons, an heirloom dating from the 1800s, is a butterhead that is both delicate and beautiful—its outer leaves are brushed with deep maroon. Butterhead lettuce dressed with a good-quality truffle oil and just a smidgen of Champagne vinegar, sea salt, and freshly ground white pepper makes an astonishingly good salad.

ROMAINE OR COS

Romaine lettuce forms an upright head, with elongated leaves that are slightly spoon shaped. The leaves may be lightly ruffled at the ends, and the center rib may or may not be pronounced. Romaines are typically quite sturdy and crunchy. Little Gem, a short, compact romaine, known in France as Sucrine, has leaves that are small enough to use whole. Cut the heads in half lengthwise, brush with extra-virgin olive oil, season with salt and pepper, and grill them. The grilling caramelizes them slightly and brings out their sweet flavor. I like to serve them directly off the grill, topped with anchovies and Parmesan cheese, or goat cheese and prosciutto.

LOOSE-LEAF

Loose-leaf lettuces grow in a loose, open shape with no discernible head. In the garden, these are sometimes called cut-and-come-again lettuces because gardeners can cut the leaves as needed and more leaves will grow. Red-leaf, green-leaf, and the Italian Lolla Rossa lettuce fall into the loose-leaf category. The fluffy, ruffled leaves have a mild flavor and make a good salad or garnish for a sandwich.

TOMATO SUMMER SALAD

*I could eat a juicy, peak-of-summer tomato salad every day.
Sometimes sliced on a platter, sometimes quartered into a bowl, any
color, any kind of tomato—it all works for me. Add some sea salt
and a good-quality extra-virgin olive oil, plus basil or parsley leaves,
whole or chopped,, and you've created a very satisfying summer plate.*

BIG-BATCH ROASTED TOMATO SAUCE

We grow a substantial number of tomatoes in our garden each year, usually three or four rows of twenty-five plants, which we put into the ground in April, if we're on schedule. One of the reasons we grow a lot of tomatoes is because we like to pick big batches of them in late August and September when they are at their peak of flavor and roast them to make sauce, which we then freeze. If we've done our job correctly, the frozen sauce will last us until the new crop of tomatoes arrives sometime the following July. You can use any kind of tomatoes to make this sauce, but the plum varieties, like San Marzano, which have a very high pulp-to-moisture ratio, yield the largest amount of sauce per pound (500 g). The juicier slicers, such as Brandywine and Cherokee Purple, or even the farmers' market standby, Early Girl, render more liquid and need a longer cooking time to thicken. I make this sauce in a big roasting pan, the same one I use for turkey, and I fill it to the brim with tomatoes.

Preheat the oven to 400°F (200°C).

Put the tomatoes into a roasting pan, stacking them if necessary. Sprinkle them with the basil, thyme, shallot, and garlic. Drizzle the oil over the top and sprinkle with 1 teaspoon of the salt and the pepper. Roast the tomatoes until they are soft and collapsing, 40–60 minutes.

Using an immersion or upright blender or a food processor, purée the tomatoes until smooth. Taste and adjust the seasoning. Strain the sauce through a chinois or fine-mesh sieve to remove the seeds and any bits of skin. Discard the solids. Taste and add more salt, if desired.

Refrigerate for up to 4 days, or ladle into any size freezer-safe lock-top plastic bags and freeze for up to 1 year. To thaw, place in a pan of cold water for several hours or place in a bowl in the refrigerator overnight.

MAKES 3–4 QT
(2.8–3.8 L)

10 lb (5 kg) ripe
summer tomatoes, cored

1 cup (1 oz/30 g) fresh
basil leaves, chopped

1 tsp fresh thyme
leaves, chopped

¼ cup (1½ oz/45 g)
minced shallot

2 cloves garlic, minced

¼ cup (2 fl oz/60 ml)
extra-virgin olive oil

1–2 tsp sea salt

1 tsp freshly
ground pepper

TOMATO TART with
WHOLE ROASTED GARLIC CLOVES

I was served a version of this tomato tart at a tiny French bistro. A couple ran the off-the-beaten-track spot; she did the cooking while he tended the bar, and both of them pitched in to serve us. This tomato tart was one of the first-course options on the prix-fixe menu that evening, followed by a second course of braised lamb with flageolet beans, and for dessert, a choice of flan, apple tart, or ice cream. I've been back many times and have yet to be disappointed. Although the instructions are for a rectangular tart pan, a 9-inch (23-cm) round fluted tart pan can be substituted.

Preheat the oven to 300°F (150°C). Place racks in the upper and lower thirds of the oven.

Drizzle just enough oil on a rimmed baking sheet to thinly coat the bottom. Sprinkle the salt, pepper, and herbes de Provence over the oil. Place the tomatoes, cut side down, on the baking sheet, rubbing them around to absorb the oil and seasoning.

Place the garlic cloves on a piece of aluminum foil, drizzle with some oil, and turn to coat evenly. Seal the foil into a packet and place it in a small baking dish.

Place the baking sheet with the tomatoes on the upper rack of the oven and the garlic on the lower rack. Roast the tomatoes until their skins slip off easily, about 15 minutes. Remove the baking sheet with the tomatoes from the oven and set aside to cool. Raise the oven temperature to 350°F (180°C) and continue to roast the garlic until soft and easily pierced with the tip of a knife, about 25 minutes longer. Set aside to cool.

When the tomatoes are cool enough to handle, remove and discard the skins, leaving the tomatoes on the baking sheet. When the garlic cloves are cool enough to handle, remove and discard the skins, leaving the cloves whole. The tomatoes and the garlic can be prepared a day ahead and stored, covered, in the refrigerator. Bring to room temperature before using.

continued on next page

SERVES 10 AS AN APPETIZER, 4–5 AS A MAIN COURSE

Extra-virgin oil for drizzling

½ tsp sea salt

½ tsp freshly ground pepper

½ tsp herbes de Provence

8–10 Roma or San Marzano tomatoes, cored and halved lengthwise

12 large cloves garlic, unpeeled

1 sheet frozen puff pastry (about ½ lb/250 g), thawed

2 tsp crème fraîche

1 tsp Dijon mustard

Raise the oven temperature to 400°F (200°C).

On a floured work surface, roll the puff pastry into a rectangle about 10 by 13 inches (25 by 33 cm). Drape it over an 8-by-11½-inch (20-by-29-cm) rectangular fluted tart pan with a removable bottom and gently press the pastry into the pan, letting the edges hang over the sides. Using your fingers, tuck the excess dough under to make a folded rim that rises slightly above the sides of the tart pan.

Line the pastry with aluminum foil and add pie weights or dried beans. Bake on the middle rack of the oven until the exposed edges begin to turn golden, about 10 minutes. Remove the weights and foil. Prick the bottom of the pastry with a fork and continue to bake until the crust turns a pale bisque, about 3 minutes longer. If it puffs up, prick the puff with a fork to deflate it. Let the crust cool slightly.

Reduce the oven temperature to 375°F (190°C).

In a bowl, combine the crème fraîche and mustard. Using a spatula, spread the mustard mixture evenly over the bottom of the tart shell.

Arrange the tomatoes, cut side up, across the surface of the tart shell. Tuck the garlic cloves among the tomatoes. With a pastry brush, brush the tops of the tomatoes with juices from the baking sheet. Bake until the edges of the crust are puffed and deep gold and the bottom is cooked through, 15–20 minutes.

Remove from the oven. Let stand for 15 minutes. Slip a knife around the edges of the pan to loosen any clinging bits of pastry. Gently push on the bottom of the pan, nudging the sides loose. Slide the tart onto a serving plate, cut into pieces, and serve warm.

HANGING GREEN TOMATOES

At the end of tomato season, before the first frost arrives and kills the plants, my neighbors in Provence pull the vines still thick with unripe tomatoes and hang them on wires strung in their *caves*, or "cool cellars," often with dirt floors. Slowly, all but the greenest and most immature fruits ripen, turning red within a month or two.

I like to think of it as nature's way of ripening green tomatoes before the invention of ethylene chambers. Granted, they won't taste like a ripe tomato picked in high summer, but they do extend the garden harvest. Of course, not everyone has a *cave*, but a basement, garage, or even a closet will work.

ZUCCHINI & PINE NUT FRITTERS

In Provence, summer gardens are laden with zucchini. They are a key ingredient in soupe au pistou *(page 42) and ratatouille, and they are frequently sautéed with lots of garlic and onion as a side dish. Here, the zucchini are grated raw, which preserves their fresh, green flavor. Similar to potato pancakes but with a softer interior, the fritters get added texture from toasted pine nuts and a sprinkle of sea salt. I like to serve these as a first course or a side dish.*

Grate the zucchini on the large holes of a grater-shredder. With your hands, squeeze out the excess liquid from the zucchini. You should have about 2 cups (10 oz/315 g).

Put the zucchini in a large bowl, sprinkle with the flour, and turn with a spoon or your hands to mix well. Add the egg, ½ teaspoon salt, and the pepper. With a spoon, mix well to form a batter.

Pour just enough oil into a frying pan to thinly coat the bottom and heat over medium-high heat. When it is hot, spoon about 3 tablespoons of the batter into the pan for each fritter, spacing them about 2 inches (5 cm) apart. With the back of a spatula, press each fritter until it is about ¼ inch (6 mm) thick. Cook until the bottoms are golden and the edges are set, 3–4 minutes. Sprinkle a few pine nuts on top of each fritter, gently pressing them in with the back of the spatula, then flip the fritters and cook until crisp and golden on the second side, about 3 minutes longer. Transfer to a paper towel–lined platter. Repeat with the remaining batter, adding more oil to the pan as needed to prevent sticking.

Scatter the remaining pine nuts over the fritters and sprinkle with salt. Serve at once.

MAKES 8–10
FRITTERS

2 zucchini

¼ cup (1½ oz/45 g) all-purpose flour

1 large egg

½ tsp coarse sea salt, plus salt for sprinkling

¼ tsp freshly ground pepper

Extra-virgin olive oil for frying

¼ cup (1¼ oz/35 g) pine nuts, toasted

CULTIVATE YOUR BLOSSOMS

Squash blossoms are almost as important to the
summer table as the squashes themselves. Some
varieties of zucchini have even been developed
just for their extra-large blossoms, but any squash
blossoms can be used. They are best picked early
in the morning while they are fully open. Check
to make sure they harbor no bees before plucking
them. Gently rinse the blossoms, wrap them in a
damp paper towel, and store them in a plastic bag
until ready to use. They don't keep well, so they
should be used within 1 or 2 days of being picked.

To prepare the blossoms simply, tuck a teaspoon
or two of filling, such as seasoned goat or ricotta
cheese, deep into the heart of the blossom, then
twist together the petals to close. In a frying pan,
heat a little olive oil over medium-high heat.
When it is hot, lay the blossoms in the pan,
but don't crowd them. Fry until golden, turning
once, about 2 minutes, then transfer to a paper
towel–lined plate or platter. Sprinkle with
coarse sea salt and serve at once. The stems,
by the way, are also delicious.

GRANDE SOUPE au PISTOU

Soupe au pistou *is the beloved late summer and fall vegetable soup of Provence that features the fresh shelling beans everyone has been anticipating all summer long. It's also laced with* pistou, *an unctuous basil purée. Here, I've used fresh cranberry and butter beans, but you can make the soup with dried cranberry or round butter beans instead, similar to those called* coco blanc *in France. Cook the dried beans in water with a bay leaf and salt until tender, about 2 hours, then add 2½ cups (17 oz/530 g) drained cooked beans and a few tablespoons of the broth to the soup with the spaghetti.*

To make the *pistou*, coarsely chop the garlic, then, using a mortar and pestle or a bowl and a wooden spoon, crush the garlic and salt into a paste. Add the basil leaves, a few at a time, and crush them into the paste. Add the oil in a thin stream and continue to stir and crush the mixture until it thickens and takes on a green tint. Set aside.

To make the soup, in a large saucepan or soup pot, heat the oil over medium-high heat. When it is hot, add the onion and sauté until translucent, 2–3 minutes. Add the potatoes, carrot, and zucchini and stir several times. Add 4 cups (32 fl oz/1 l) water, the broth, thyme, parsley, and salt and bring to a boil. Reduce the heat to medium, cover, and simmer until the carrot and potatoes are tender, 15–20 minutes.

Meanwhile, trim the haricots verts and cut into 1-inch (2.5-cm) lengths. Add the cranberry and butter beans to the soup and cook until nearly tender to the bite, about 15 minutes. Break the spaghetti into 1-inch (2.5-cm) lengths and add them to the pot with the haricots verts. Cook until the spaghetti is tender, 8–10 minutes. With the back of a fork, crush some of the potatoes and cranberry and butter beans to thicken the soup.

Discard the thyme and parsley sprigs and taste and adjust the seasoning. Pour the soup into a tureen or serving bowl and stir in 2 tablespoons of the *pistou*. Serve at once, with the remaining *pistou* on the side.

SERVES 6

for the pistou

3–4 cloves garlic

¼ tsp coarse sea salt

1 cup (1 oz/30 g) fresh basil leaves

⅓ cup (3 fl oz/80 ml) extra-virgin olive oil

for the soup

1 Tbsp extra-virgin olive oil

1 small yellow onion, diced

3 boiling potatoes, peeled and diced

1 carrot, peeled and diced

1 large zucchini, diced

3 cups (24 fl oz/750 ml) chicken broth, homemade (page 166) or purchased

4 fresh thyme sprigs

4 fresh parsley sprigs

1 tsp sea salt

½ lb (250 g) haricots verts

1 lb (500 g) fresh cranberry beans in the pod, shelled

1 lb (500 g) fresh butter beans in the pod, shelled

2 oz (60 g) dried spaghetti

EGGPLANTS STUFFED
with RICE & SAUSAGE

Eggplants, which thrive in the Mediterranean climate, are featured in many different dishes in the countries that border the sea. In southern France, they are regularly stuffed with a variety of fillings and then baked. I make a sausage-rice mixture for my stuffing, which is especially easy when I have a little leftover rice. Instead of rice, I sometimes use 1 cup (2 oz/60 g) bread cubes, soaked in milk and squeezed dry. I like to serve this dish with Big-Batch Roasted Tomato Sauce (page 33).

Preheat the oven to 350°F (180°C).

Cut the eggplants in half lengthwise, leaving the green cap and stem intact. Scoop out the flesh from the eggplant halves to create a shell about ½ inch (12 mm) thick. Finely chop the eggplant flesh.

In a bowl, combine the sausage, chopped eggplants, onion, garlic, parsley, thyme, pepper, salt, and egg and mix well with your hands. Add the rice and mix again.

To check the seasoning of the sausage mixture, form a small patty and fry it in a small frying pan over medium-high heat until cooked. Taste and adjust the seasoning of the uncooked sausage mixture if needed.

Divide the sausage mixture among the eggplant shells, mounding the tops. Place the stuffed eggplants on a rimmed baking sheet and bake until the eggplant is tender when pierced with the tip of a knife and the stuffing is golden brown and cooked through, 35–40 minutes.

Serve hot or at room temperature.

SERVES 4

4 eggplants

1 lb (500 g) mild Italian bulk sausage

½ yellow onion, minced

2 cloves garlic, minced

2 Tbsp minced fresh flat-leaf parsley leaves

2 Tbsp minced fresh thyme leaves

1 tsp freshly ground pepper

½ tsp sea salt

1 large egg

1 cup (5 oz/155 g) cooked long-grain white rice, at room temperature or cold

ROASTED BEET, BLUE CHEESE,
& WILD ARUGULA SALAD

You'll notice a distinct, earthy aroma when roasting beets, which is one of the reasons I especially like roasting them rather than boiling or steaming them. This salad's combination of sharp, wild arugula and soft blue cheese, all dressed with a walnut oil vinaigrette, signals fall for me. Try to find beets with the leafy greens still attached, which means they have been freshly dug. They will have a fuller flavor than the leafless beets that have been in cold storage.

Preheat the oven to 350°F (180°C).

Arrange the beets in a single layer in a baking dish. Add the olive oil, ½ teaspoon of the salt, and the pepper and turn several times to coat well. Roast until the beets are easily pierced with the tines of a fork, 1 hour or more, depending on their size. Set aside to cool.

When the beets are cool enough to handle, remove and discard the skins with your fingers or a paring knife. Cube or slice the beets.

In a salad bowl, whisk together the walnut oil, vinegar, and the remaining ¼ teaspoon salt. Add the arugula and half of the beets and toss to coat well. Arrange the arugula mixture on a platter and top with the remaining beets and the blue cheese. Serve at once.

SERVES 4–6

4 beets, any variety, trimmed

2 tsp extra-virgin olive oil

¾ tsp sea salt

½ tsp freshly ground pepper

1 Tbsp walnut oil

1 tsp sherry vinegar

4 cups (4 oz/125 g) wild arugula leaves

2 oz (60 g) soft blue cheese such as bleu d'Auvergne or Gorgonzola, crumbled or cut into small pieces

GRILLED PERSIMMON, WALNUT & GOAT CHEESE SALAD

In the village of Quinson, not far from my house in Provence, there is a huge persimmon tree that I have watched grow for more than thirty years. By November, its orange fruits are brilliant against the ocher of the old stone house and a vineyard framed by a forest. At my house in California, we planted two persimmon trees nearly twenty years ago; they're almost as tall as the tree in Quinson and equally beautiful, though without the Provençal landscape. One of my trees is the Fuyu type, which is the firm, flattish one, and the other is a chocolate type, which, although we eat it out of hand, can sometimes be bitter. Throughout the season, I use the Fuyu persimmons for salads and for slicing and grilling to serve with meats and poultry.

Cut the persimmons crosswise into ¼-inch (6-mm) slices. Remove the seeds, if any. Brush the persimmon slices on both sides with 1 teaspoon of the olive oil.

Heat a grill pan over medium-high heat. When it is hot, grill the persimmons until lightly golden, 1–2 minutes per side. Transfer to a cutting board and cut each slice into 4–6 bite-size wedges. Set aside.

In a salad bowl, whisk together the remaining olive oil, the vinegar, walnut oil, salt, and pepper. Add the arugula and toss to coat well. Add half of the persimmons, half of the walnuts, and half of the goat cheese and toss again.

Arrange the arugula mixture on a platter and top with the remaining persimmons, walnuts, and goat cheese. Serve at once.

SERVES 4–6

4 Fuyu persimmons

3 Tbsp extra-virgin olive oil

2 tsp sherry vinegar

1 tsp walnut oil

¼ tsp sea salt

¼ tsp freshly ground pepper

2 cups (2 oz/60 g) baby arugula leaves

½ cup (2 oz/60 g) walnut halves or pieces, toasted

4–5 oz (125–155 g) soft goat cheese, crumbled

PUMPKIN GALETTES with FRIED SAGE

In fall, the big, deeply lobed, copper-burnished pumpkin known as Musquée de Provence comes to the markets of southern France, where it is sold by the wedge. The flesh is dark orange, dense, and has a mildly nutty flavor. Happily, it is now available in the fall at many farmers' markets and supermarkets. Seeds are available from various sources online if you'd like to grow your own. It can be baked, steamed, puréed, or given just about any treatment. Here, roast pumpkin is mixed with egg and flour to make savory galettes that are crisp on the outside and creamy on the inside. They can serve as a main course, though I also like them as a side dish with merguez sausage (page 170).

Preheat the oven to 350°F (180°C).

Slice the pumpkin into 3-inch (7.5-cm) wedges and scrape out and discard any seeds and stringy threads from the cavity. Place the wedges on a rimmed baking sheet, drizzle with the oil, sprinkle with 1 teaspoon of the salt and ½ teaspoon of the pepper, and toss to coat. Roast until the pumpkin wedges are easily pierced with the tines of a fork, about 1 hour. Set aside to cool.

Using a large spoon, scrape the cooled flesh into a large bowl and discard the skins. Squeeze out and discard any excess moisture with your hands, then add the egg and beat with the spoon. In a small bowl, whisk together the flour, baking powder, and the remaining 1 teaspoon sea salt and ½ teaspoon pepper. Add to the pumpkin mixture and stir to make a wet batter.

Pour a thin coating of oil into a large frying pan and heat over medium-high heat. When hot, spoon about ¼ cup (2 fl oz/60 ml) batter into the pan for each galette, spacing them 1 inch (2.5 cm) apart. With the back of a wooden spoon, flatten each galette into a thin disk. Cook, turning once, until golden brown on both sides, about 4 minutes per side. Transfer to a plate and keep warm.

Pour oil to a depth of ¼ inch (6 mm) into a small frying pan and heat over high heat. Add the sage leaves and fry, turning once or twice, until crisp, 4–5 seconds. Transfer to a paper towel to drain.

Top the galettes with the sage, sprinkle with coarse salt, and serve.

MAKES 8–10 GALETTES; 4 SERVINGS

2–2½-lb (1–1.25-kg) wedge *Musquée de Provence* pumpkin, or 1 Sugar Pie pumpkin or butternut squash

2 Tbsp extra-virgin olive oil, plus oil for frying

2 tsp sea salt

1 tsp freshly ground pepper

1 large egg

1 cup (5 oz/155 g) all-purpose flour

¼ tsp baking powder

Leaves from 8–10 fresh sage sprigs

¼–½ tsp coarse sea salt

SWEET PEPPER &
SHELLING BEAN GRATIN

Fresh shelling beans have only a short season, in late summer and early fall, when the pods are shriveled and the plump beans inside are still tender. If you can find fresh beans, use them. If not, substitute dried cranberry beans that have been cooked with a little salt, a bay leaf, and winter savory or thyme. The base of this simple dish is the combination of shelling beans and onions with fall's sweet bell peppers. Chunks of bread lightly fried in olive oil are scattered across the top. I find this gratin substantial enough to serve as a main course, but it could also serve as a dressed-up side dish for leg of lamb. If you are cooking a leg of lamb or other roast, enrich the peppers and beans with a tablespoon or two of the jus.

To prepare the beans, shell the beans, then bite into 1 or 2 beans to test the freshness. If the beans offer a little resistance, but not much, they will cook in about 20 minutes. If they're tough or hard to bite through, they can take up to 35 minutes. You should have about 3 cups (1 lb/500 g).

In a large pot, combine 6 cups (48 fl oz/1.5 l) water, the bay leaf, winter savory, salt, and pepper and bring to a boil over medium-high heat. Add the beans, reduce the heat to medium, and cook, uncovered, until the beans are soft and tender to the bite, 20–35 minutes. Let the beans stand in their cooking liquid until ready to use.

To prepare the peppers and onion, in a frying pan, heat the oil over medium-high heat. When it is hot, add the onion, reduce the heat to medium, and cook until slightly soft, about 3 minutes. Add the bell peppers and cook, stirring occasionally, until the onion and peppers are very soft, about 15 minutes. Do not let them brown.

Preheat the oven to 400°F (200°C). Drain the beans and reserve the cooking liquid. Remove and discard the bay leaf and winter savory sprig.

continued on next page

SERVES 4

for the beans

2–2½ lb (1–1.25 kg) cranberry, borlotto, or other shelling bean in the pod

1 fresh or ½ dried bay leaf

1 fresh winter savory or thyme sprig

1 tsp sea salt

½ tsp freshly ground pepper

for the peppers & onion

¼ cup (2 fl oz/60 ml) extra-virgin olive oil

½ yellow onion, thinly sliced

1 red bell pepper, seeded and cut lengthwise into thin strips

1 yellow or orange bell pepper, seeded and cut lengthwise into thin strips

➡→

50.

La Vie Rustic

Pour the onion, bell peppers, and their cooking juices into a 4-cup (1-l) gratin dish. Add the beans and 1–2 tablespoons of the reserved cooking liquid and stir several times to combine. Add the meat *jus* (if using), ½ tablespoon of the oregano, and the salt, pepper, cumin, and saffron. Taste and adjust the seasoning. Set aside.

To make the topping, cut the crust from the bread. Tear the bread into bite-size pieces.

Drizzle just enough oil into a frying pan to thinly coat the bottom and heat over medium-high heat. When it is hot, add the bread and sauté until lightly golden on all sides, about 3 minutes. Sprinkle with the salt. With a slotted spoon, transfer the fried bread bits to the gratin dish, scattering them over the beans, onion, and peppers.

Bake until the gratin is bubbling and the topping is golden brown, about 15 minutes. Remove from the oven and sprinkle with the remaining ½ tablespoon oregano.

Serve at once, or let cool for 10–15 minutes and serve warm.

2 Tbsp meat *jus* (optional)

1 Tbsp chopped fresh oregano

¼–½ tsp sea salt

¼–½ tsp freshly ground pepper

¼ tsp ground cumin

⅛ tsp saffron threads

for the topping

4-inch (10-cm) piece baguette or coarse country bread

Extra-virgin olive oil for frying

¼ tsp sea salt

THE LAST PEPPERS

Sweet peppers, such as Corno di Toro, Cuneo, and blocky bell pepper types, are not as susceptible to frost as tomatoes. They can be left on the vine longer, where they will mature into a deep, sweet red, even as their plants begin to senesce. The fruit's skin may begin to wrinkle a bit, but that doesn't affect their flavor. So even though it's tempting to clear out the peppers along with the tomatoes as you get ready to plant a fall or winter crop, leave them in the ground a little bit longer. It's worth it.

CARAMELIZED LEEK FLATBREAD
with BLACK OLIVES & SOFT CHEESE

A quintessential offering at every boulangerie in Provence, pissaladière is a pizza-like dough spread with a thick layer of deeply caramelized onions and dotted with oil-cured olives and anchovies. I've eaten it many times for breakfast at a café, along with a steaming café crème. This flatbread is similar, with its somewhat chewy crust, and the caramelized leeks are even sweeter than onions. You could add anchovies, too, if you wanted.

To make the dough, dissolve the yeast in the warm water, then add the sugar and let stand until foamy, about 5 minutes.

In a food processor, combine the yeast mixture, 2½ cups (12½ oz/390 g) of the flour, 2 tablespoons of the oil, and the salt. Pulse, adding more flour ¼ cup (1½ oz/45 g) at a time, just enough to create a soft ball of dough—not too sticky, not too dry. When you touch the dough, it should not stick to your fingers.

Knead the dough on a floured work surface with your hands until smooth and elastic, about 7 minutes. Form the dough into a smooth ball.

Rub a large bowl with 1 tablespoon of the oil. Place the kneaded dough ball in the bowl and turn to coat the dough with the oil. Cover the bowl with a damp kitchen towel and let the dough rise in a warm, draft-free spot until doubled in size, 1½–2 hours.

To prepare the leeks, trim the roots and the dark green upper parts and discard. Cut the leeks in half lengthwise and thoroughly wash before chopping. Finely chop the pale green and white parts.

continued on next page

SERVES 4

for the dough

1 package (2½ tsp) active dry yeast

1 cup (8 fl oz/250 ml) warm water (105°F/40°C)

½ tsp sugar

2¾–3 cups (14–15 oz/440–470 g) all-purpose flour, plus flour for dusting

3 Tbsp (2 fl oz/60 ml) extra-virgin olive oil, plus oil for brushing

1 tsp sea salt

➡

In a frying pan or sauté pan with a lid, heat the 2 tablespoons oil over medium-high heat. When it is hot, add the leeks, salt, and pepper. Stir several times, then cover and reduce the heat to low. Cook, stirring occasionally, until the leeks are lightly golden, 35–40 minutes. Set aside. (If not using right away, cover and refrigerate for up to 1 day.)

Place a pizza stone or a heavy baking sheet in the oven and preheat the oven to 500°F (260°C).

Punch down the dough and transfer it to a floured work surface, turning it over once. Roll it into a 15-by-12-inch (38-by-30-cm) oval about ½ inch (12 mm) thick. Lightly dust a baking sheet with a little flour. Partially drape the rolled-out dough over the rolling pin and unroll it onto the baking sheet.

With a spatula, spread the leeks over the dough, leaving a ½-inch (12-mm) uncovered border around the edges. Dot the leeks with the goat cheese and the olives. Brush the edges of the crust with olive oil.

Bake until the crust is puffed and golden along the edges and the bottom is crisp and golden, about 15 minutes.

Remove from the oven, and while still hot, brush the edges once again with olive oil. Cut into pieces and serve at once.

for the leeks

2 large leeks

2 Tbsp extra-virgin olive oil

½ tsp sea salt

¼ tsp freshly ground pepper

3 oz (90 g) soft goat cheese, farmer cheese, or other fresh, soft cheese

12–15 oil-cured black olives, pitted

Extra-virgin olive oil for brushing

SAVORY CHARD & RAISIN PIE

I first learned to make Swiss chard pie, a specialty of the area around Nice and its backcountry, while living in Saorge, a mountain village not far from the Italian border. Like many regional dishes, the chard and raisin pie has many incarnations, some sweet and some savory. This one can be served as a light main dish or a first course, or it can be cut into bite-size pieces and speared on toothpicks as an appetizer. I usually have chard growing in my garden, and while I most often steam it or use it in gratins, I find this versatile tart a lovely way to use more of it.

Preheat the oven to 375°F (190°C).

Cut out the stems and ribs from the chard and reserve for another use. Stack several chard leaves on top of one another, roll up tightly, and slice thinly into chiffonade.

Pour 2 cups (16 fl oz/500 ml) water into a soup pot or large casserole, add the chard and bacon, and cover. Bring to a boil over medium-high heat, then reduce the heat to medium and cook until the chard is tender and wilts to about half of its original volume, about 15 minutes. Drain the chard, discard the bacon, and set the chard aside to cool. When it is cool enough to handle, squeeze out the excess liquid with your hands. Chop the chard, squeeze again, and set aside.

Heat a frying pan over medium-high heat and add the sausage, breaking it up into smallish pieces with a spoon or spatula. Sauté the sausage, stirring often, until opaque but not browned, about 8 minutes. With a slotted spoon, transfer to a paper towel–lined plate to drain.

In the same frying pan, sauté the onion and garlic in the sausage drippings over medium heat until soft and translucent, about 2 minutes. Transfer to the plate with the sausage.

Drain the raisins. In a large bowl, stir together the chard, sausage, onion mixture, Parmesan cheese, pine nuts, raisins, whole egg, salt, and pepper. Set aside.

continued on next page

SERVES 8 AS AN
APPETIZER, 4–6
AS A MAIN COURSE

5 large or 10 medium chard leaves

1 slice thick-cut bacon, chopped

1 lb (500 g) bulk pork sausage

½ yellow onion, finely chopped

1 clove garlic, minced

1 Tbsp raisins, soaked in 1 cup (8 fl oz/250 ml) water

¼ cup (1 oz/30 g) freshly grated Parmesan cheese

3 Tbsp pine nuts

1 large whole egg plus 1 large egg yolk

¼–½ tsp sea salt

¼ tsp freshly ground black pepper

Double recipe Lard Pastry (page 183) or purchased pie dough for one double-crust 9-inch (23-cm) pie

On a floured work surface, roll out half of the pastry dough into an 11-inch (28-cm) circle. Drape it over a 9-inch (23-cm) pie pan and gently press the pastry into the pan, letting the edges hang over the sides. Do not trim the overhang; it will be trimmed later.

Line the pastry with aluminum foil and add pie weights or dried beans. Bake until the exposed edges begin to turn pale bisque, 7–8 minutes. Remove the foil and weights. Prick the bottom of the pastry with a fork and bake until the crust turns a pale bisque, 3–4 minutes. If it puffs, prick the puff with a fork to deflate it. Let the crust cool slightly, about 5 minutes. Gently fill the pastry shell with the chard mixture, spreading it evenly.

Roll out the remaining pastry dough into a 10-inch (25-cm) circle. With a pastry brush, brush water around the rim of the lower pastry shell, then gently lay the second pastry round over the top, letting the edges hang over the sides. Press the edges of the pastry together, sealing them. Don't worry if some of the lower pieces break off; they will eventually be trimmed. Once the top is secure, cut out a circle ½ inch (12 mm) in diameter in the middle to allow steam to escape. Trim the edge of the top and bottom crusts, leaving a ½-inch (12-mm) overhang, then fold the overhang under to create an attractive edge.

In a small bowl, lightly beat together the egg yolk and 1 tablespoon water. With a pastry brush, brush the top of the pie with the egg wash. Place the pie pan on a rimmed baking sheet and bake until the crust is golden and the sides begin to pull away slightly from the sides of the pan, about 25 minutes.

Remove from the oven and let stand for at least 30 minutes. Cut into wedges and serve warm or at room temperature.

WHITE BEAN &
WINTER SAVORY SOUP

Take good-quality large dried white beans, like Royal Coronas, season them with sweet bay leaves and winter savory, and you'll have an exceptionally satisfying soup—one in which the broth is as good as the beans. Winter savory, which grows wild in Provence, is reminiscent of thyme and rosemary, but different. It is an essential ingredient in herbes de Provence, is used to season goat cheese, and is a favorite for seasoning beans. If you like, add some cooked sausages or meat from a cooked ham hock toward the end of cooking. Beans can be soaked overnight to reduce the cooking time, or they can be simply cooked without soaking. I prefer the latter, but either method results in a delicious soup. Serve this hearty soup with crusty bread for dipping into the broth.

Pick over the beans, discarding any misshapen beans, stones, or other odd particles. Rinse under running cold water and drain. Put the beans in a large soup pot and add water to cover by 3 inches (7.5 cm). Add the bay leaves and bring to a boil over medium-high heat. Reduce the heat to low, cover, and simmer for 1 hour.

Uncover the pot and add 1 teaspoon of the salt, ¼ teaspoon of the pepper, the winter savory sprigs (if using), and ¼ teaspoon of the dried winter savory. Stir, re-cover the pot, and continue to cook until the beans are almost tender to the bite, about 1 hour longer.

Uncover the pot and add the remaining 1 teaspoon salt and the remaining ¼ teaspoon dried winter savory. Stir, re-cover the pot, and continue to cook until the beans are completely tender, up to 1 hour longer. The beans are done when they are completely tender and offer no resistance to the bite. Taste and adjust the seasoning with salt and pepper. Remove and discard the bay leaves and winter savory sprigs. Serve at once.

SERVES 6

1 lb (500 g) dried
Royal Corona beans or
other large white beans

2 fresh or 1 dried bay leaf

2 tsp sea salt, plus more
to taste

¼ tsp freshly ground
pepper, plus more to taste

2 fresh winter savory
sprigs (optional)

½ tsp dried
winter savory

CELERY ROOT & POTATO PURÉE
TOPPED with PANFRIED SWEETBREADS

This is what I call French farmhouse comfort food. Hot, creamy, buttery root vegetable purée, topped with lightly fried nuggets of sweetbreads and then eaten in front of a roaring fire with a glass of local red wine, is my idea of cozy. Sweetbreads must be soaked, cleaned, and then soaked twice more. Although these steps are time-consuming, the result is worth the effort.

Put the sweetbreads in a large bowl and add cold water to cover. Add ¼ cup (2 fl oz/60 ml) of the lemon juice and let soak for 1 hour or so. Using your fingers, separate the sweetbreads into lobes and remove the white membranes. Drain the sweetbreads and repeat the soaking step two more times, using fresh water only. Drain a final time and rinse with cold running water.

Place the sweetbreads in a large saucepan and add cold water to cover by 1 inch (2.5 cm). Add the remaining 2 tablespoons lemon juice and bring to just below a boil over medium-high heat. Reduce the heat to low and poach for 15 minutes. Drain and let cool to room temperature. Cut into 1-inch (2.5-cm) slices.

Put the potatoes and celery roots in a large saucepan and add water to cover by 2 inches (5 cm). Add 1 tablespoon salt and bring to a boil over medium-high heat, then reduce the heat to medium and cook until tender, about 20 minutes. Drain and return the potatoes and celery root to the hot pot. Add the milk and 6 tablespoons (3 oz/90 g) of the butter and mash together. Taste and adjust the seasoning and add more milk, if desired. Keep warm.

Preheat the oven to 250°F (120°C). In a frying pan, heat the remaining 2 tablespoons butter and the oil over medium heat. On a plate, stir together the bread crumbs, 2 teaspoons salt, and 1 teaspoon pepper. Coat the sweetbread slices evenly with the crumbs. Working in batches, fry the sweetbread slices, turning often, until golden, about 5 minutes. Keep warm in the oven until serving.

Divide the vegetable purée among dinner plates and top with the sweetbreads. Serve at once.

SERVES 4–6

2 lb (1 kg) sweetbreads

¼ cup (4 fl oz/125 ml) plus 2 Tbsp fresh lemon juice or white vinegar

1½ lb (750 g) Yukon gold potatoes, peeled or unpeeled, cut into 1-inch (2.5-cm) pieces

1 large or 2 medium celery roots, peeled and cut into 1-inch (2.5-cm) pieces

Sea salt and freshly ground pepper

½ cup (4 fl oz/125 ml) whole milk, plus milk if needed

½ cup (4 oz/125 g) unsalted butter, cut into small pieces

1 Tbsp grapeseed oil

1 cup (1½ oz/45 g) fresh bread crumbs or 1 cup (1¾ oz/55 g) panko bread crumbs

SPINACH à la CRÈME

I could eat spinach every day. Plain spinach, buttered spinach, and, above all, creamed spinach. However, not all spinach is created equal. Savoyed-leaf varieties, with their puckered leaves and thick stems, are the ones you want to use for this creamed spinach. Usually sold in bulk at farmers' markets everywhere, the sturdy leaves hold their own in this dish, while the thin, flat-leaved varieties tend to disappear in the cream. One of my neighbors in France, sadly now passed away, always kept a big patch of savoyed-leaf spinach growing during fall and winter. She would make huge gratins of creamed spinach all season long. Here is a quicker, easier version for the stove top. Savoyed varieties trap grit more easily; be sure to rinse the leaves well before cooking.

If the spinach stems are thick and fibrous, remove and discard them; otherwise, leave them intact. Thoroughly wash the spinach in several changes of water, then immerse it in a pot or bowl of cold water. With your hands, pick up the wet spinach and transfer it to a large pot. Sprinkle with 1 teaspoon salt and cover the pot.

Bring the spinach to a boil over medium heat. It will release its moisture as it cooks. Reduce the heat to medium-low and cook until the spinach is tender to the bite and thoroughly wilted, about 15 minutes. The amount of cooking time depends on the type of spinach, with sturdy savoyed types taking longer to cook than thin, smooth-leaved types.

Drain the spinach and set aside to cool. When the spinach is cool enough to handle, squeeze out the excess liquid with your hands. Coarsely chop the spinach and squeeze again.

In a sauté or frying pan, melt the butter over medium-high heat. When it foams, add the cooked spinach, 1 teaspoon salt, ½ teaspoon pepper and cook, stirring, for 1–2 minutes. Sprinkle with the flour and stir until incorporated. Slowly pour in about ½ cup (4 fl oz/125 ml) of the cream, stirring, and cook until a sauce forms, about 6 minutes. Taste and adjust the seasoning. If the sauce seems too thick, add up to ¼ cup (2 fl oz/55 ml) more cream.

Transfer to a serving dish and serve at once.

SERVES 2-3

2 lb (1 kg) sturdy spinach, preferably a savoyed-leaf variety such as Bloomsdale

Sea salt and freshly ground pepper

4 Tbsp (2 oz/60 g) unsalted butter

2 Tbsp all-purpose flour

½–¾ cup (4–6 fl oz/125–180 ml) heavy cream

½ tsp freshly ground pepper, plus pepper to taste

CHICORY SALAD with
SAUTÉED CHICKEN LIVERS

One of the specialties of the Burgundy region around Mâcon is escarole salad with
sautéed chicken livers. I first had it late one evening at a Mâcon brasserie where my
husband and I met friends after a long trek down from Paris. We didn't want a big
dinner, as it was already 10 p.m., but we were hungry. A salad, one with some heft,
sounded just right—and it was. Since that night, I've made it many times, often with
mixed chicories from the garden, such as Castelfranco, Chioggia, Palla Rossa, and
Treviso radicchio, along with escarole. The greens, all from the same botanical family,
form a slightly bitter base that sets off the sweetness of the sautéed livers and shallot.

To make the vinaigrette, in a salad bowl, whisk together
the oil, vinegar, salt, and pepper. Set aside.

To prepare the chicken livers, pick over them and remove
any fatty pieces and dark veins. In a large frying pan, heat
the butter and oil over medium-high heat. When they are hot,
add the shallot and sauté just until translucent, 1–2 minutes.
With a slotted spoon, transfer the shallot to a bowl. Add the
chicken livers to the pan, sprinkle them with the salt and
pepper, and sauté, turning frequently, until the livers are
firm to the touch and still have a faint rose hue when cut
open, about 8 minutes. Be careful not to overcook them.
Return the shallot and any juices to the pan and stir once
or twice, just to combine. Remove from the heat.

Add the chicories to the bowl with the vinaigrette and toss
to coat well. Divide the chicories between 2 dinner plates
or large shallow bowls. Top with the chicken livers, shallot,
and a little of the pan juices. Serve at once.

SERVES 2

for the vinaigrette

3 Tbsp extra-virgin
olive oil

1 Tbsp red wine vinegar

¼ tsp sea salt

¼ tsp freshly
ground pepper

for the chicken livers

10 oz (315 g)
chicken livers

1 Tbsp unsalted butter

1 Tbsp extra-virgin
olive oil

3 Tbsp minced shallot

½ tsp sea salt

¼ tsp freshly
ground pepper

3 cups (3 oz/90 g) torn
leaves of assorted
chicories such as
Castelfranco, Chioggia,
Palla Rossa, and Treviso
radicchio and escarole

PARSNIP SOUP with TOASTED ALMONDS

Before the potato was introduced to Europe by way of South America, parsnips were the main starchy vegetable of the Continent. Like potatoes, parsnips are extremely versatile and can be roasted, baked, fried, steamed, or boiled. They are also inherently sweet. For this soup, I've played on that sweetness by adding apple and onion, bringing it all into balance with a little lemon.

In a heavy-bottomed saucepan, heat the oil over medium-high heat. When it is hot, add the parsnips, potato, apple, onion, salt, and pepper and sauté, stirring frequently, until the vegetables and apple start to caramelize and soften, 10–15 minutes. Add the sherry and deglaze the pan by scraping up any bits that cling to the bottom. Add 3 cups (24 fl oz/750 ml) water and bring to a boil. Reduce the heat to medium and cook, loosely covered, until the flavors blend and the soup thickens, about 15 minutes.

Using an immersion or upright blender, purée the soup just until smooth. Stir in the lemon juice. Taste and adjust the seasoning. If necessary, reheat before serving.

In a small bowl, stir together the almonds and lemon zest. Ladle the soup into bowls and sprinkle with the almond–lemon zest mixture. Serve at once.

SERVES 4

2 Tbsp extra-virgin olive oil

2 large parsnips, peeled and cut into ½-inch (12-mm) cubes

1 russet potato, peeled and cut into ½-inch (12-mm) cubes

1 apple such as Gala or Golden Delicious, peeled, cored, and cut into ½-inch (12-mm) cubes

¼ cup (1 oz/30 g) chopped yellow onion

½ tsp sea salt

½ tsp freshly ground pepper

2 Tbsp dry sherry

¼ tsp fresh lemon juice

¼ cup (1½ oz/45 g) whole almonds, toasted and chopped

1 Tbsp sliced lemon zest, in 1-inch (2.5-cm) slivers

CREAMY CELERY ROOT SOUP

This is a soup to go all out for and to enjoy, and please, do not worry about the cream. The celery root flavor is pure and intense — better than celery — and this elegant dish is sumptuous enough to be the first course of a special dinner party.

In a heavy-bottomed soup pot or stockpot, melt the butter over medium heat. When it foams, add the celery root, leeks, celery, and shallot and cook, stirring occasionally, until the leeks and shallot are translucent, about 2 minutes. Sprinkle with the salt and red pepper flakes to taste and stir once or twice. Add the wine, raise the heat to medium-high, and bring to a boil. Scrape up any bits that cling to the bottom of the pot and continue to boil until most of the liquid has evaporated, about 5 minutes. Add the broth and bring to a boil, then reduce the heat to medium-low, cover, and simmer until the celery root is soft and easily pierced with the tines of a fork, 15–20 minutes.

Using an immersion or upright blender, purée the soup until smooth. Transfer to a clean pot and stir in the cream. Bring to a gentle simmer over medium-low heat and cook until the soup has a creamy consistency, about 5 minutes. For an exceptionally smooth soup, place a chinois or fine-mesh sieve over yet another clean pot and strain the soup, gently pressing any remaining solids with the back of a spoon. Gently simmer to reheat once again, if needed.

Serve at once.

SERVES 6

3 Tbsp unsalted butter

2 lb (1 kg) celery root, peeled and cut into 1-inch (2.5-cm) cubes

4 leeks, white parts only, chopped

3 ribs celery, including leaves, chopped

1 shallot, minced

1 tsp sea salt

$\frac{1}{8}$–$\frac{1}{4}$ red pepper flakes or $\frac{1}{8}$ tsp cayenne pepper

$\frac{1}{2}$ cup (4 fl oz/125 ml) dry white wine

5 cups (40 fl oz/1.25 l) chicken broth, homemade (page 166) or purchased

1 cup (8 fl oz/250 ml) heavy cream

POTATO & MERGUEZ CHOWDER
with HARICOTS ROUGES

*I like the French name for the large pink and black bean we call scarlet runner:
haricot rouge d'Espagne. The beautiful scarlet blossoms are a highlight in the
potager, and the plants produce long, wide pods that can be eaten fresh, like green
beans, once the tough strings are cut away. Left on the vine to dry, the pods turn buff
colored and need to be harvested before they shatter. Here, I cook the dried beans and
then simmer them with little meatballs of merguez and with new potatoes for a
hearty winter soup. If you wish, soak the beans overnight to reduce the cooking time.*

Pick over the beans, discarding any misshapen beans, stones,
or other odd particles. Rinse under running cold water and
drain. Put the beans in a large soup pot and add water to cover
by 3 inches (7.5 cm). Add the bay leaves and bring to a boil
over medium-high heat. Reduce the heat to low, cover, and
simmer for 1 hour.

Uncover the pot and add 1 teaspoon of the salt, the winter
savory sprigs, and ¼ teaspoon of the dried winter savory.
Stir, re-cover the pot, and continue to cook until the beans
are almost tender to the bite, about 1½ hours longer.

Uncover the pot and add the remaining 1 teaspoon salt and
the remaining ¼ teaspoon dried winter savory. Stir, re-cover
the pot, and continue to cook until the beans are completely
tender, up to 1 hour longer. The beans are done when they are
completely tender and offer no resistance to the bite. Taste and
adjust the seasoning, adding more salt, if desired, and the pepper.
Let the beans stand in their cooking liquid until ready to use.
(If not using right away, leave the beans in their cooking liquid,
cover, and refrigerate for up to 1 day.)

Preheat the oven to 350°F (180°C).

continued on next page

SERVES 4–6

½ lb (250 g) dried
scarlet runner beans
or red kidney beans

2 fresh or 1 dried bay leaf

2 tsp sea salt

3 fresh winter savory
or thyme sprigs

½ tsp dried winter savory

¼ tsp freshly
ground pepper

➥

If using purchased *merguez* sausage, remove and discard the casing. Shape the sausage into ½-inch (12-mm) meatballs and arrange on a rimmed baking sheet. Bake, turning once or twice, until golden brown and cooked through, 15–20 minutes. Remove from the oven and set aside.

Drain the beans through a fine-mesh sieve, capturing the cooking liquid in a bowl or a large measuring pitcher. Discard the bay leaves and winter savory sprigs.

In a Dutch oven, melt the butter over medium-high heat. When it foams, add the celery and onion and sauté until soft and translucent, about 2 minutes. Add the potatoes, stir several times, then add the broth and the tomatoes and their juice. Bring to a boil, then add 1 cup (8 fl oz/250 ml) of the reserved bean cooking liquid. Reduce the heat to medium and simmer until the potatoes are nearly tender, about 20 minutes. Transfer 2 cups (16 fl oz/500 ml) of the soup to a blender and purée until smooth. Return the puréed mixture to the soup along with 1½ cups (10½ oz/330 g) of the cooked beans and the cooked meatballs and simmer until the flavors blend, 5–10 minutes.

Ladle the soup into bowls. Serve at once.

1 lb (500 g) *merguez* sausage, homemade (page 170) or purchased

1 Tbsp unsalted butter

4 ribs celery, chopped

½ yellow onion, finely chopped

2 red potatoes, unpeeled, cut into 1-inch (2.5-cm) cubes

2½ cups (20 fl oz/625 ml) beef or chicken broth, homemade (page 166) or purchased

1 cup (8 oz/250 g) canned plum tomatoes, chopped, with their juice

WINTER BEIGNETS with SAUCE VERTE

Winter provides some exceptional vegetables that lend themselves well to deep-frying. Cardoons, parsnips, celery root, and Jerusalem artichokes are the ones I like best for this technique, but you could use carrots, cauliflower, and broccoli florets as well. The batter I dip them in is quite light, similar to a tempura batter, and the spicy green sauce that I serve alongside them, thick with capers and green herbs, disappears as fast as the beignets do.

To make the *sauce verte*, combine the parsley, ¼ cup (2 fl oz/60 ml) of the oil, the green onions, capers, shallot, tarragon, lemon juice, garlic, and salt in a blender or food processor and process until a thick paste forms. With the motor running, slowly drizzle in the remaining ½ cup (4 fl oz/120 ml) oil and process until a thick sauce forms. Taste and adjust the seasoning. (If not using right away, cover the sauce with a little olive oil to maintain its bright green color and refrigerate for up to 1 day.)

To make the beignets, trim the root end of each cardoon stalk. With a sharp knife, cut off any leaves and stickery edges. Using a vegetable peeler, peel the curved backs of the stalks to remove the outer layer of skin and any tough strings. Cut the stalks into 3-inch (7.5-cm) pieces and rinse them in running cold water.

Combine 3 cups (24 fl oz/750 ml) water, the milk, and 1 tablespoon of the salt in a saucepan and bring to a boil over medium-high heat. When it is boiling, add the cardoons, reduce the heat to medium, and cook until the cardoons are easily pierced with the tines of a fork, 30–40 minutes Remove them with a slotted spoon and set them aside. Discard the cooking liquid. This step can be done up to 1 day ahead, and the cardoons covered and refrigerated.

continued on next page

SERVES 4–6

for the *sauce verte*

1 cup (1 oz/30 g) fresh flat-leaf parsley leaves, coarsely chopped

¾ cup (6 fl oz/180 ml) extra-virgin olive oil

½ cup (1½ oz/45 g) chopped green onions, white and pale green parts

¼ cup (2 oz/60 g) capers

2 Tbsp minced shallot

2 Tbsp coarsely chopped fresh tarragon

1 Tbsp fresh lemon juice

1 clove garlic, minced

¼ tsp sea salt

→

Peel the parsnips and cut the thick upper half lengthwise into 4 equal pieces, then cut again to make ¼-inch (6-mm) *batonnets*. Leave the narrow lower half of the root whole. Peel the Jerusalem artichokes and slice them lengthwise into ¼-inch (6-mm) slices.

Preheat the oven to 200°F (95°C). Line a platter with paper towels.

Pour the grapeseed oil into a heavy-bottomed saucepan or deep fryer to a depth of 3–4 inches (7.5–10 cm) and heat over medium-high heat until it reaches 360°F (185°C) on a deep-frying thermometer.

While the oil heats up, make the beignet batter. In a tall glass or a bowl, combine the ice cubes and 1½ cups (12 fl oz/375 ml) water. Set aside. In a bowl, combine the 1¼ cups (5 oz/155 g) flour, the egg yolk, and the remaining ½ teaspoon salt. Remove the ice cubes from the water and discard them. Measure out 1 cup (8 fl oz/250 ml) of the ice water and add it to the flour mixture, whisking together until a batter forms.

Sprinkle 1 cup (4 oz/125 g) cake flour on a plate. Dredge the vegetable pieces, a few at a time, in the flour and then dip them in the batter. Add to the hot oil and fry, turning once or twice, until golden, about 2 minutes. With a slotted spoon, transfer to the prepared platter. Season lightly with a little salt. Keep warm in the oven while you deep-fry the remaining vegetables.

Serve at once, with the *sauce verte* on the side.

for the beignets

1 lb (500 g) cardoons

1 cup (8 fl oz/250 ml) whole milk

1 Tbsp plus ½ tsp sea salt, plus salt for seasoning

2 parsnips

3 Jerusalem artichokes

Grapeseed or canola oil for deep-frying

4–5 ice cubes

1¼ cups (5 oz/155 g) cake flour, plus about 1 cup (4 oz/125 g) flour for dredging

1 large egg yolk

WARM JERUSALEM ARTICHOKE SALAD with LARDONS

The French consider Jerusalem artichokes (also known as sunchokes) to be a forgotten vegetable. But on a recent trip to Paris, I noticed that they appeared on menus throughout the city; it seems the knobby root has been rediscovered. A Jerusalem artichoke is the root of a tall plant that looks a lot like a sunflower, and it has a sweet, starchy taste and crunchy white flesh. It can be eaten raw or cooked. Here, I use it both raw and cooked, balancing it with peppery watercress for constrast. I maintain its crunch by just barely sautéing it in a bit of the fat from the lardons.

To make the vinaigrette, in a salad bowl, whisk together the oil and vinegar, followed by the mustard, salt, and pepper. Set aside.

To make the salad, peel and thinly slice the Jerusalem artichokes crosswise, then halve or quarter the slices, depending upon their size.

In a frying pan, sauté the lardons over medium-high heat until they are nearly crisp and have rendered their fat, about 6 minutes. With a slotted spoon, transfer the lardons to a paper towel–lined plate.

Pour off all but 1 tablespoon of the fat from the pan. Add the onion to the pan and cook over medium-high heat until softened, about 2 minutes. Add half of the Jerusalem artichokes and sauté just long enough to warm through and soften a bit, about 2 minutes longer.

Add half of the sautéed Jerusalem artichokes, half of the raw Jerusalem artichokes, half of the watercress, and all of the lardons to the bowl with the vinaigrette and toss gently to coat well.

Arrange the remaining watercress sprigs on 4 salad plates. Top with the salad mixture, garnish with the remaining sautéed and raw Jerusalem artichokes, and serve.

SERVES 4

for the vinaigrette

1½ Tbsp extra-virgin olive oil

1½ tsp sherry vinegar

1½ tsp Meaux or Dijon mustard

¼ tsp sea salt

¼ tsp freshly ground pepper

for the salad

6 Jerusalem artichokes, about 1½ lb (750 g) total

3 oz (90 g) lardons, or 3 slices thick-cut bacon, cut crosswise into ¼-inch (6-mm) slices

1 Tbsp minced yellow onion

2 cups (2 oz/60 g) watercress sprigs (about 1 bunch), tough stems removed

CARDOON & BONE MARROW GRATIN

A member of the thistle family and closely related to the artichoke, the cardoon is an ancient vegetable prized in the kitchen for its thick stalks, which look like outsized celery ribs. It is attractive in the garden, with its tall stature and its deeply notched, silvery leaves. Cardoons are in markets from December into February and are popular among Italians as well as the French. The innermost stalks and the heart of the plant are thinner and more tender than the outer stalks. A gratin of cardoons is one of the classic dishes of le gros souper, *the traditional Christmas Eve dinner of Provence (page 126). For a meatless version, substitute ½ cup (4 oz/125 g) butter for the bone marrow, though the bone marrow makes the dish especially unctuous.*

Trim the root end of each cardoon stalk. With a sharp knife, cut off any leaves and the stickery edges. Using a vegetable peeler, peel the curved backs of the stalks to remove the outer layer of skin and any tough strings. Cut the stalks into 3-inch (7.5-cm) pieces and rinse them in running cold water.

Combine 4 cups (32 fl oz/1 l) water, 2 cups (16 fl oz/500 ml) of the milk, and 1 tablespoon of the salt in a saucepan and bring to a boil over medium-high heat. When it is boiling, add the cardoons, reduce the heat to medium, and cook until the cardoons are easily pierced with the tines of a fork, 30 to 40 minutes. Remove them with a slotted spoon and set aside. Discard the cooking liquid.

Preheat the oven to 375°F (190°C). Butter an 11-by-7-by-2-inch (28-by-18-by-5-cm) baking dish with 2 teaspoons of the butter.

Fill a large bowl with ice water and soak the marrowbones for 10 minutes to draw out any residual blood. Remove the bones, pat dry, and set aside.

In a saucepan, melt the remaining 2 tablespoons butter over medium-high heat. When it foams, remove the pan from the heat and whisk in the flour. Return the pan to medium-high heat and whisk in the remaining 2 cups (16 fl oz/500 ml) milk, a little bit at a time, until combined. Reduce the heat to medium, add the

SERVES 4–6

2 lb (1 kg) cardoons, preferably 2 small

4 cups (32 fl oz/1 l) whole milk

1 Tbsp plus ½ tsp sea salt

2 tsp plus 2 Tbsp unsalted butter

4 beef marrowbones, each 6–8 inches (15–20 cm) long, halved lengthwise by your butcher

2 Tbsp all-purpose flour

¼ tsp freshly ground pepper

¼ tsp freshly grated nutmeg

2 cups (8 oz/250 g) shredded Gruyère or Emmentaler cheese

remaining ½ teaspoon salt, the pepper, and nutmeg and cook until the sauce thickens to a creamy consistency like a béchamel, about 15 minutes.

Lay half of the cardoons in the bottom of the prepared baking dish and cover with half of the cheese. Scoop the marrow out of 2 of the bones, cut it into small pieces, and scatter the pieces randomly on top of the cheese. Repeat with the remaining cardoons, cheese, and marrow. Pour the hot sauce over the top.

Bake until the cheese melts, the sauce bubbles, and the top is golden, about 20 minutes. Serve at once, directly from the baking dish.

BLANCHING CARDOONS

The cardoon is definitely an old-fashioned vegetable, one that takes some work before it reveals its tender, delicious self (see left and page 73). If you decide to grow cardoons—large plants with long, arching, frilly-leaved stalks of gray, much like artichokes—in your garden, you will need to blanch them before harvesting. Blanching is a gardening technique in which one or more parts of a plant are covered to prevent the sun from reaching them, keeping them pale and tender. This technique is often applied to escarole and frisée as well as cardoons. One or two cardoon plants will suffice for most households.

Heres how to blanch your cardoons: Use gloves and long sleeves to protect yourself from the plant's sharp spines. When the stalky leaves are about 2 feet (60 cm) high, pound in a 3-foot (1-m) wooden stake next to the plant. Wrap sheets of heavy craft paper or corrugated cardboard around the lower 1 foot (30 cm) of the plant, then fasten the sheets tightly with twine. Tie the wrapped plant to the stake to help prevent it from falling over.

After 3 weeks, the stalks and inner heart of the cardoon plant will be blanched and ready to be harvested and used in the kitchen. The craft paper or cardboard will get wet when it rains, but unless the rains are prolonged and relentless, it will dry out and continue to do its job. Plastic, as tempting as it is, is not a good choice for blanching because it heats up the plant and traps moisture.

CHAPTER TWO

THE ORCHARD

THE ORCHARD

FRUITS & NUTS

THE FRENCH HAVE AN INHERENT NOTION OF BALANCE THAT IS DISPLAYED IN THEIR HOME ORCHARDS AND VINEYARDS, WHERE BEAUTY AND PRACTICALITY ARE ONE AND the same. There is no line, no separation between ornamental and edible.

Flowering fruit trees provide the first colors of spring, and the silver leaves of olive trees shimmer year-round. Tidily pruned grapevines give structure to a small yardscape.

As winter moves to spring, the trees and vines leaf out and begin to bear the first fruits of the season: cherries, mulberries, apricots, and peaches. These are made into tarts, cooked in savory dishes, and served, day after day, as a conclusion to every meal in lieu of a sweet confection. As the season moves into summer, plums and figs appear on the table, to be followed by fall's grapes, pears and apples, quinces and persimmons. Nuts ripen in fall, too, and are ready for the picking. Grapes and apples are crushed and fermented, and olives are picked and cured or turned into olive oil at the local mill.

As fall's cool temperatures turn the leaves of trees and vines into shades of gold and red, the colors of a different palette come to the yardscape. Once the leaves fall, the symmetry of bare branches creates yet another vision of a practical yet ornamental space.

Most home orchards in France are not large. They may include just a few fruit trees and grapevines, or perhaps there's a nut tree or two planted along the house or in a community garden. This can be done where you live (see page 281 for instructions on creating your own *potager* and orchard).

A friend in suburban Northern California has a small backyard where she tends a cherry tree, fig tree, olive tree, orange tree, lemon tree, and two grapevines. This small orchard supplies her kitchen with fresh fruit daily, when in season, and plenty of surplus fruit to preserve; she even cures her own olives.

In my own home orchards, my trees have varied from a single orange tree and pomegranate tree to a long row of Meyer lemons, many orange trees, and singleton trees of apricots, apples, figs, plums, and pears, plus enough olive trees to take fruit to the olive mill.

The home orchard, perhaps a grand term for just a few fruit and nut trees and grapevines, is an integral part of the simple, sustainable way of life that has evolved in France. Even a modest orchard enhances the visual space of a home as well as supplies the kitchen with an abundance of fresh food.

HOME-CURED CRACKED GREEN OLIVES

Olives must be cured to leach out their bitterness. Various methods are used, including packing them in ashes, using lye, dry salting, and soaking in brine or water. Once they are cured, they are put in brine with seasonings or packed in olive oil. Marie, a neighbor in France, taught me the water method used here. Every day I went to the cave *(cellar) with her to change and taste the olive water to gauge the bitterness level. Choose firm, slightly shiny olives without a hint of blush for curing. If the skin is still matte, they were picked too soon. Dried winter savory can be used for the fresh, or you can double the number of thyme sprigs. Fennel is found wild in many areas or can be cultivated. Look for the flower heads from summer into fall.*

Using a mallet or the back of a wooden spoon, gently hit each olive just to crack the flesh; be careful not to crush the olive or break the pit, or the final product might be mushy. Put the olives in a nonreactive crock, vat, or pot, add cold water to cover, then cover the container with several layers of cheesecloth. For 5 pounds (2.5 kg), I like to use my pasta pot with its strainer insert. Put the pot in a cool, dark place. The next day, change the water. When using the pasta insert, I simply lift it out with the olives, pour out the water, replace the insert, and refill the pot with cold water to cover the olives. Change the water every day in this manner for at least 10 days, or up to 25 days. Start tasting the olives after 10 days. They will be bitter, but gradually the bitterness will diminish, though some will always remain.

When most of the bitterness is gone, the olives are ready to be brined. To make the brine, combine 4 qt (4 l) water, the vinegar, salt, fennel, winter savory, thyme, bay leaves, orange peel, coriander seeds, and peppercorns in a stockpot. Cook over medium-high heat, stirring, until the salt dissolves, about 3 minutes. Reduce the heat to medium and cook, uncovered, for 15 minutes longer. Remove from the heat and let cool completely.

Pack the olives into 1-pt (16–fl oz/500-ml) jars. Strain the brine, then pour it into each jar to within ½ inch (12 mm) of the rim. Cap tightly. Store in the refrigerator for at least 1 week before eating. The olives will keep for 3 months.

MAKES TEN 1-PINT (16–FL OZ/500-ML) JARS

5 lb (2.5 kg) fresh green medium or large olives, any variety

1 cup (8 fl oz/250 ml) white wine vinegar

¾ cup (6 oz/185 g) coarse sea salt

1 flowering fennel head or ½ tsp fennel seeds

2 fresh winter savory sprigs or ½ tsp dried winter savory

2 fresh thyme sprigs

2 fresh or 1 dried bay leaf

1-inch (2.5-cm) piece dried orange peel

½ Tbsp coriander seeds

½ Tbsp black peppercorns

CRISPY FRIED OLIVES

Olives are at the heart and soul of life in southern France. Everyone who can has at least one or two olive trees, and whenever possible, a small grove, which is enough to make a few liters of oil. Most people are adept at curing their own olives (page 85), and those who aren't always make sure their pantries have plenty on hand to serve with aperitifs and for cooking. These crispy fried olives are a fancied-up appetizer to serve with drinks. I usually include them as part of a charcuterie platter with slices of jambon cru (French-style prosciutto), hard cheese and honey, and toasted walnuts. Any variety of olive is delicious here, but large green ones are exceptionally good.

In a small bowl, whisk together the eggs. Strain them through a fine-mesh sieve to remove any stringy threads.

If you want a more refined appearance for your fried olives, process the panko in a food processor or blender, or use a rolling pin to crush them between 2 sheets of plastic wrap or aluminum foil.

Place the panko crumbs in a shallow bowl or on a plate. Place the flour in another shallow bowl or on a plate. Drain the olives.

Pour the oil into a heavy-bottomed saucepan to a depth of 1–1½ inches (2.5–4 cm) and heat over medium-high heat until it reaches 375°F (190°C) on a deep-frying thermometer.

Dip several olives at a time into the egg, then dip them into the flour, gathering them back through your fingers and shaking off the excess flour. Dip them into the panko the same way, gathering them back through your fingers and shaking off the excess. Dip again into the egg, followed by the panko, shaking off the excess.

With a slotted spoon, slide the olives into the hot oil. Fry until the bottom is golden and crispy, about 1 minute, then roll them over and fry the second side until golden and crispy, about 1 minute longer. Transfer to a paper towel–lined plate to drain. Repeat until all of the olives are fried. Serve at once.

SERVES 4–6

2 large eggs

1 cup (1¾ oz/55 g) panko bread crumbs

1 cup (5 oz/155 g) all-purpose flour

24 pitted olives, any kind

Grapeseed or canola oil for frying

CLASSIC TAPENADE & SOCCA

Tapenade, the quintessential olive spread that's beloved in Provence, is easy to make at home. You can prepare it with different types of olives, sometimes with nuts, and with varying seasonings. This recipe combines both black and green olives and traditional seasonings, but feel free to experiment. The tapenade goes perfectly with socca, *the chickpea flour crepe of Nice and one of France's great street foods, now offered on restaurant menus. I serve the crepes torn, rather than cut, into pieces accompanied by this tapenade, the way I once had them at an Oliviers et Co. restaurant in Forcalquier. A round of soft goat cheese is a nice addition to the table.*

To make the tapenade, coarsely chop the olives, transfer to a food processor or blender, and add the anchovies, capers, and thyme. Process until chopped, about 2 minutes. With the motor running, slowly drizzle in 2 tablespoons of the oil and process until a stiff paste forms, adding more oil if needed to achieve a good spreading consistency. Cover and refrigerate until ready to use, up to 3 days.

To make the *socca*, sift the chickpea flour into a bowl. Whisk in the pepper and salt, then slowly pour in the warm water, whisking the batter until there are no lumps. Whisk in 2 tablespoons of the oil. Cover and refrigerate for several hours, overnight, or up to 2 days. The batter is quite forgiving.

To cook the crepes, in a 10-inch (25-cm) frying pan, heat about 1 tablespoon of the oil over medium-high heat. When the oil is hot, stir the batter well, then pour just enough of it into the pan to thinly coat the bottom. Cook until the edges brown and curl slightly, about 2 minutes. It will be similar to a traditional crepe but sturdier. Flip and cook the second side until the edges brown and curl slightly, about 2 minutes longer. Transfer to a paper towel–lined platter to keep warm. Repeat with the remaining batter, adding more oil to the pan as needed to prevent sticking.

Serve the warm crepes, whole or torn into pieces, with the tapenade.

MAKES ABOUT
6 CREPES;
SERVES 4–6

for the tapenade

1 cup (5 oz/155 g) pitted oil-cured black olives

1 cup (5 oz/155 g) pitted brine-cured green olives such as Picholine

2 anchovy fillets in olive oil, drained and chopped

1 Tbsp capers

1½ tsp fresh thyme leaves

2–4 Tbsp extra-virgin olive oil

for the socca

1 cup (3¼ oz/95 g) chickpea flour

1½ tsp freshly ground pepper

1 tsp sea salt

1 cup (8 fl oz/250 ml) warm water (105°F/40°C)

4–6 Tbsp (2–3 fl oz/60–90 ml) extra-virgin olive oil

PISTACHIO & BEET SALAD with GOAT CHEESE & PISTACHIO OIL

Pistachios have become popular in France, as has good pistachio oil. The quality of the oil can be verified by its golden green color; it should also be redolent at first whiff of the taste of pistachios. When drizzled over sweet roasted beets and paired with nutty arugula, the match seems just right. If you want to make this a main-course salad, add thin slices of smoked duck breast, a little more oil, and just a tiny bit more sea salt.

Preheat the oven to 350°F (180°C). Line a baking dish or rimmed baking sheet with aluminum foil.

Cut off the beet tops. Trim off and set aside a few of the smaller leaves for adding to the salad and reserve the larger leaves for another use. (They are excellent braised, for example.) Scrub the beets, quarter them lengthwise, and then halve them cross-wise. The pieces should be bite size. Arrange the beets snugly in a single layer in the prepared baking dish. Drizzle with the oil, sprinkle with the ½ teaspoon salt, and turn several times to coat.

Roast, turning several times, until tender and easily pierced with the tines of a fork and a bit crispy on the edges, 45–60 minutes. Set aside to cool to room temperature.

Arrange the arugula and reserved small beet leaves on 4 salad plates. Divide the beets evenly among the plates, crumble the goat cheese over the top, and finish with the nuts. Drizzle 1½ teaspoons of the pistachio oil over each salad and sprinkle with salt. Alternatively, arrange the salad on a single platter and serve family-style. Serve at once.

SERVES 4

6 beets, preferably red or Chiogga, with tops

1½ Tbsp extra-virgin olive oil

½ tsp coarse sea salt, plus salt for sprinkling

15 young arugula leaves

3–4 oz (90–125 g) soft goat cheese

½ cup (2 oz/60 g) pistachios in the shell, shelled, toasted, and coarsely chopped

2 Tbsp pistachio oil

PEAR, ARUGULA &
SHAVED PARMESAN SALAD

Pears are considered one of the most elegant fruits, some with buttery flesh, others slightly grainy, with skin colors ranging from reds and russets to golds and greens. They are delicate, and only a handful of varieties are cultivated on a commercial scale because so many of the others don't hold up under the duress of shipping and handling. The home orchardist, of course, does not have those same worries, which makes it possible to choose from among hundreds of other varieties. Pears, unlike many other fruits, cannot be left to ripen on the tree or the flesh becomes mushy. Pick pears that are slightly underripe, place them in a paper bag on your kitchen counter, and let them ripen to perfection. Nearly any pear variety can be used in this simple salad, which balances sweet and salty flavors.

In a salad bowl, whisk together the oil, vinegar, salt, and pepper. With a vegetable peeler, shave long, wide ribbons from the chunk of cheese. You'll need about 16 ribbons.

Add the arugula to the bowl with the vinaigrette and toss well to coat. Place one-quarter of the dressed arugula on each of 4 salad plates, heaping it into a mound.

Cut the pears in half lengthwise and carefully remove the core from each half. Cut the halves lengthwise into paper-thin slices. Place the pear slices and the Parmesan ribbons around and on top of the heaped arugula, alternating them as you go. Serve at once.

SERVES 4

3 Tbsp extra-virgin olive oil

1½ Tbsp balsamic vinegar

¼ tsp sea salt

¼ tsp freshly ground pepper

1 chunk Parmesan cheese, about ¼ lb (125 g)

4 cups (4 oz/125 g) wild arugula leaves

2 pears, any variety

FLATBREAD ROLLED with OLIVES, JAMBON CRU & TOMATO CONFIT

This flatbread uses the same all-purpose dough as the Caramelized Leek Flatbread with Black Olives and Soft Cheese (page 53), but the dough is rolled more thinly. Any kind of cured meats, herbs, vegetables, and cheeses can be used. For the olives, I suggest Mediterranean-style cured olives or brined types like Picholine or Kalamata for the best flavor. Slices of the stuffed flatbread, which look like pinwheels, can be served as hors d'oeuvres or a light main course. The whole roll is eminently transportable for a picnic or potluck and can be sliced on-site and then eaten out of hand.

Preheat the oven to 275°F (135°C).

Cut the tomatoes lengthwise into quarters, or into halves if small, and place them on a rimmed baking sheet. Drizzle with 1 tablespoon of the oil and sprinkle with ¼ teaspoon of the salt and the pepper.

Bake until the tomatoes have collapsed and turned somewhat jammy, about 30 minutes. Set aside to cool. When cool enough to handle, coarsely chop. (If not using right away, cover and refrigerate for up to 1 day.)

Dissolve the yeast in the warm water, then add the sugar and let stand until foamy, about 5 minutes.

In a food processor, combine the yeast mixture, 2½ cups (12½ oz/390 g) of the flour, 2 tablespoons of the oil, and the remaining 1 teaspoon salt. Pulse, adding more flour ¼ cup (1½ oz/45 g) at a time, just enough to create a soft ball of dough—not too sticky, not too dry. When you touch the dough, it should not stick to your fingers.

Knead the dough on a floured work surface with your hands until smooth and elastic, about 7 minutes. Form the dough into a smooth ball.

continued on next page

SERVES 4–6
AS AN APPETIZER

4 plum tomatoes

4 Tbsp (2 fl oz/60 ml) extra-virgin olive oil, plus oil for brushing

1¼ tsp sea salt

¼ tsp freshly ground pepper

1 package (2½ tsp) active dry yeast

1 cup (8 fl oz/250 ml) warm water (105°F/40°C)

½ tsp sugar

2¾–3 cups (14–15 oz/440–470 g) all-purpose flour, plus flour for dusting

3-oz (90-g) piece *jambon cru*

½ cup (2½ oz/75 g) olives, pitted and coarsely chopped

¼ cup (⅓ oz/10 g) chopped fresh basil

¼ cup (1 oz/30 g) freshly grated Parmesan cheese

Rub a large bowl with the remaining 1 tablespoon oil. Place the kneaded dough ball in the bowl and turn to coat the ball with the oil. Cover the bowl with a damp kitchen towel and let the dough rise in a warm, draft-free spot until doubled in size, 1½ to 2 hours.

Place a pizza stone or a heavy baking sheet in the oven and preheat the oven to 500°F (260°C).

Punch down the dough and transfer to a floured work surface, turning it over once. Roll it into a 15-by-12-inch (38-by-30-cm) rectangle about ¼ inch (6 mm) thick. (Reserve any excess dough for another use.) Prick the surface all over with the tines of a fork. Lightly dust a baking sheet with a little flour and set aside.

Thinly cut the *jambon cru* into 6 slices, each about 4 by 2 inches (10 by 5 cm). With a spatula, spread the tomato confit over the dough, leaving a ½-inch (12-mm) uncovered border around the edges. Sprinkle the olives over the dough, then lay 2 slices of the *jambon cru* end to end along each of the long edges, then the final 2 slices down the middle. Do not worry if the *jambon cru* doesn't completely cover the dough, as a few gaps are okay. Sprinkle with the basil.

With a short side facing you, roll the dough away from you, jelly-roll fashion, making sure the roll is snug and tight. When fully rolled, brush the dough edge with water, then pinch the seam to seal. With water on your fingertips, pinch the ends closed.

Gently lift the roll with both hands and transfer it to the prepared baking sheet. Brush the roll with oil and sprinkle with half of the Parmesan cheese. Bake for 8 minutes, then brush the roll with oil again and return to the oven. Bake until the crust and bottom are golden brown, 7–8 minutes.

Remove from the oven and brush again with oil and sprinkle with the remaining Parmesan cheese. Let stand for 5 minutes.

Using a serrated knife, cut into 1-inch (2.5-cm) slices. Serve hot or warm.

APPLES & QUINCES STUFFED with SAUSAGE, CELERY & WALNUTS

Quinces are a particular favorite of mine. I started my quince trees—really more like unruly shrubs—from cuttings my husband acquired from an old homestead in Northern California where a Spanish family had lived for decades. A little water and sun and soon we had stick-like quince trees growing along our garden fence. Now, ten years later, they are more than twice my height. When they bloom, they have soft, delicate pink flowers, and the fruit turns yellow-gold when ripe. I first cooked quinces from an old tree of my French neighbor's—a failed attempt at making quince paste. However, I discovered that quinces could be used in savory ways, too, just like apples. These savory stuffed fruits make a tasty main dish for the chilly days of fall and winter.

Preheat the oven to 350°F (180°C).

Cut a thin slice off the top of each quince and apple. Using a small metal spoon, scoop out the seeds and most of the flesh from each fruit to create a shell about ¾ inch (2 cm) thick. Discard the seeds and reserve the flesh. Be careful, as the quince and apple shells can break easily. Even if one does break, it is still usable, however. The filled fruits will be packed tightly against one another in the baking dish, holding them together.

Mince enough of the reserved quince and apple flesh to measure ¾ cup (3 oz/90 g). Sprinkle the inside of each quince with the sugar.

In a large bowl, stir together the minced quince and apple, sausage, celery, walnuts, raisins, and sage.

Put the quince and apple shells in a baking dish just large enough to hold them snugly. Fill each one with about one-eighth of the sausage mixture, forming it into a mound that rises about 1 inch (2.5 cm) above the rim of the fruit. Pour water into the baking dish to a depth of ½ inch (12 mm). Bake until the stuffing is cooked through and brown on the top and the shells of the fruits can easily be pierced with the tines of a fork, about 40 minutes. Serve at once.

SERVES 4–6

4 quinces

4 apples such as Golden Delicious or Gala

1 Tbsp sugar

1½ lb (750 g) bulk pork sausage

3 ribs celery, finely chopped

½ cup (2 oz/60 g) chopped walnuts

½ cup (2 oz/60 g) raisins

1½ Tbsp minced fresh sage

BLANCHED ALMONDS

Blanching your own almonds is easy to do. Raw almonds are briefly soaked in boiling water and then their thin, papery seed coats are slipped off, revealing their gleaming kernels. After being rolled in a little salt, the ivory tones glitter on the unadorned nuts. Almonds are typically harvested in late August, and the fresher the almonds, the more easily the seed coats slip off.

Put the almonds in a large bowl and pour the boiling water over them. Let stand for 1 minute, then drain. Using your fingers, gently rub the brown seed coats until they slip off the nuts. If they don't slip off easily, repeat the boiling water and rubbing process, but let the nuts stand for only 30 seconds before draining them.

Place the egg whites in a small bowl and beat with a whisk or fork until frothy but not stiff. Using a small paintbrush or your fingers, very lightly brush the egg white on each almond and then sprinkle with salt. If you use too much egg white, the salt will adhere thickly, making for a very salty—perhaps too salty—almond.

Place the salted almonds on parchment paper or aluminum foil and let dry for at least several hours, or up to overnight. Store in covered tins, boxes, or glass jars in a cool, dry place. The nuts will keep for up to 3 months.

MAKES 3 CUPS (16 OZ/500 G)

1 lb (500 g) raw almonds

8 cups (64 fl oz/2 l) boiling water

4 large egg whites

½ cup (4 oz/125 g) sea salt

NUT OILS

In the nut-producing regions of France, such as Gascony, Périgord, the Alps, and the Loire, nuts have been milled for their oil for centuries. Although many of the mills have been turned into homes or inns, quite a few are still functioning, pressing artisanal walnut, almond, and hazelnut oils in small batches. In California, nut oil featuring local walnuts, almonds, and pistachios, as well as Oregon hazelnuts, are made using traditional French milling methods. Nut oils are intense in flavor and aroma and add depth when used in salads or to season vegetables. Use a little less nut oil than you would olive oil, or even blend the nut oil with a little grapeseed oil for a milder flavor. I like to whisk walnut oil into mashed potatoes, or drizzle hazelnut oil over fresh goat cheese and top it with toasted hazelnuts and chopped dried cherries.

WALNUT & BLUE CHEESE SAUCE

Because of their high oil content, nuts make a good component in sauces. The crunch and texture of the walnuts give this versatile sauce added character and keep it from being overwhelmingly cheesy. My favorite way to serve this sauce is with gnocchi, but I also like to spoon it over freshly steamed vegetables such as broccoli, cauliflower, or green beans and then top the dish with some buttered bread crumbs.

Combine the cream, rosemary sprigs, and minced rosemary in a small saucepan and bring to a boil over medium-high heat. Cook until the cream is reduced to about ⅔ cup (5 fl oz/160 ml), about 10 minutes; it should be quite thick. Remove and discard the rosemary sprigs, then stir in the cheese and walnuts. Serve at once over pasta or vegetables.

MAKES ABOUT 1 CUP
(8 FL OZ/250 ML);
3–4 SERVINGS

1½ cups (12 fl oz/375 ml)
heavy cream

2 fresh rosemary sprigs,
plus 2 tsp minced
fresh rosemary

2 oz (60 g) soft blue
cheese such as bleu
d'Auvergne or fourme
d'Ambert, crumbled

¼ cup (1 oz/30 g) chopped
walnuts, toasted

PORK SHANK BRAISED with APPLES

Orchards are a common sight in Normandy, which is nearly as famous for its apples as for its cheeses. Apple trees are a popular choice for the home orchard because just one tree produces more than enough fruit for a family. In France, apples are classified as cider, eating, or cooking apples, though many can be used for more than one purpose. For cooking and eating, I am a fan of the old-fashioned Golden Delicious apple, which originated in the United States but has become a favorite in France.

If the pork shank has skin, use a sharp knife to score the skin in a crosshatch pattern, allowing about 1 inch (2.5 cm) between the cuts. Be careful not to cut into the meat. Pat the pork shank dry, then rub all over with the salt and pepper.

In a large, heavy-bottomed pot, melt the butter over medium-high heat. When it foams, add the shank and cook, turning once, until golden brown, about 6 minutes. Using tongs, turn the shank to brown the edges, about 2 minutes per side. Transfer the shank to a platter, leaving the rendered fat and pan juices behind.

Add the onions to the pot and sauté until translucent, 2–3 minutes. Raise the heat to high, add 2 cups (16 fl oz/500 ml) of the cider, and deglaze the pot by scraping up any bits clinging to the bottom. Reduce the heat to very low, add half of the apple slices, and top with the shank. Sprinkle with the thyme, cover, and cook, stirring occasionally, until the pork is tender when pierced, about 1½ hours. If the apples begin to stick, add a little cider. During the last 20 minutes of cooking, lay the remaining apples on the shank.

Transfer the shank to a carving board and the recently added apples to a warmed platter. Carve the shank into slices, with the skin if desired, and transfer to the platter. Cover to keep warm.

Pour off any fat from the pot, leaving any juices and the now-dissolved first apples behind. Raise the heat to high, add the remaining 1 cup (8 fl oz/250 ml) cider, and again deglaze the pot. Gradually add the butter-flour paste, stirring until the sauce thickens. Drizzle the sauce over the pork and apples and serve.

SERVES 4-6

1 pork shank, 2½–3 lb (1.25–1.5 kg), with or without skin

1 tsp sea salt

1 tsp freshly ground pepper

3 Tbsp unsalted butter

2 yellow onions, minced

3 cups (24 fl oz/750 ml) dry hard cider, plus cider as needed

4 Golden Delicious or other firm apples, peeled, cored, and cut into ½-inch (12-mm) slices

1 tsp fresh thyme leaves

1 Tbsp unsalted butter, at room temperature, mixed with 1 Tbsp all-purpose flour to make a paste

CHESTNUT & PORK RAGOUT
with GLACÉED PEARL ONIONS

Chestnuts are a harbinger of winter in France, and when the weather turns chilly and damp, street vendors appear from Paris to Nice, roasting chestnuts and offering them hot in paper cones. One of the most famous areas for chestnuts is the Massif des Maures, a coastal mountain range stretching from Hyères to Toulon. On the far side of the range, wild chestnut forests cover nearly 4,000 acres (1,630 hectares). Chestnut trees live a very long time, and some of the trees in the forests are between four hundred and five hundred years old.

Besides being roasted on streets and in homes, chestnuts are used in both sweet and savory preparations, like this stew. To accompany the stew, I serve boiled potatoes slicked with butter and parsley, or egg noodles.

Preheat the oven to 325°F (165°C).

To prepare the pork, in a large, heavy-bottomed pot, cook the fatback over low heat until the fat renders and is at a depth of ¼ inch (6 mm), about 15 minutes. If there is not enough rendered fat, add a little butter and/or oil. Remove the crisp fatback and save it for another use or discard it.

Raise the heat to medium-high. When the fat is nearly smoking, add the pork in batches, being sure not to crowd the pot, as crowding the pork will cause it to steam and prevent it from developing a nice brown crust. Season with some of the salt and pepper and cook, turning several times, until browned on all sides, about 6 minutes. Transfer to a bowl. Repeat with the remaining pork, salt, and pepper, adding more butter and/or oil to the pot if needed to prevent sticking.

Reduce the heat to medium and add the onion, leek, and thyme to the now-empty pot. Cook, stirring often, until the vegetables soften, about 2 minutes. Raise the heat to high, add the wine, and deglaze the pot by scraping up any bits that cling to the bottom.

continued on next page

SERVES 4–6

for the pork

2 oz (60 g) fatback or slab bacon, cut into 1-inch (2.5-cm) cubes

Unsalted butter and/or extra-virgin olive oil if needed

2½–3 lb (1.25–1.5 kg) boneless pork shoulder, trimmed and cut into 1½-inch (4-cm) cubes

1 tsp sea salt

½ tsp freshly ground pepper

½ yellow onion, chopped

1 large leek, white and pale green parts, chopped (about ½ cup/1½ oz/45 g)

➡

Return the pork and any juices to the pot and cook, stirring several times, over medium heat. Sprinkle the flour over the pork and stir until the pork is coated with the flour. When the flour begins to brown lightly, slowly pour in about 1 cup (8 fl oz/250 ml) of the broth, stirring constantly, to create a sauce. As the sauce thickens, slowly add the remaining 3 cups (24 fl oz/750 ml) broth, continuing to stir now and then until a thin sauce forms, about 8 minutes.

Bring to a boil, then cover and transfer to the oven. Bake, stirring from time to time and adding more broth as needed to maintain a good sauce consistency, until the meat can almost be cut with a fork, 1½–2 hours. Stir in the chestnuts and mustard, cover, and bake until the meat nearly falls apart, about 30 minutes longer.

While the ragout is cooking, prepare the onions: Cut off the tip of each onion and peel away the skin. Leave the root end intact, as this helps the onion to hold its shape during cooking. Put the onions in a small saucepan and add water to cover by about ½ inch (12 mm). Add the butter and salt and bring to a simmer over medium-high heat. Reduce the heat to medium-low, cover, and simmer until the onions offer little resistance when pierced with the tines of a fork, about 20 minutes. Remove from the heat and set aside.

Remove the pork from the oven. Reheat the onions over medium-high heat, turning them often, until they are shiny and most of the liquid has evaporated, 3–5 minutes.

Spoon the ragout into a serving bowl and scatter the onions over the top. Serve at once.

1 Tbsp fresh thyme leaves

1 cup (8 fl oz/250 ml) dry white wine such as Sauvignon Blanc

2 Tbsp all-purpose flour

4 cups (32 fl oz/1 l) pork or chicken broth, plus broth as needed, homemade (page 166) or purchased

1 lb (500 g) vacuum-packed unsweetened chestnuts

2 Tbsp Dijon mustard

for the onions

16 pearl onions

2 Tbsp unsalted butter

½ tsp sea salt

HAZELNUT FRIED CHICKEN GIZZARDS with GREENS

Hazelnuts, noisettes in French, grow wild in Normandy and in southeastern France, and the shrubby trees are often used in hedgerows around fields or alongside homes. The round nuts are rich and crunchy and are prime treats for wild collection. You can use any nuts in this salad, but since gizzards are such a typical specialty of southeastern France, I like keeping the sense of place with hazelnuts. In the United States, chicken gizzards are often packaged with hearts, and these can be used as well—just confit them along with the gizzards.

Trim the silver skin from the gizzards, then cut the gizzards in half and rinse under cold running water. Transfer to a bowl, add the juniper berries, 1 teaspoon of the salt, ½ teaspoon of the pepper, and the garlic and turn to coat. Cover and refrigerate overnight.

The next day, preheat the oven to 250°F (120°C). Place the gizzards in a small baking dish with a lid. In a small saucepan, melt 1 cup (7 oz/220 g) of the duck fat over medium heat, then pour it over the gizzards, covering them completely. If necessary, melt more duck fat. Cover the dish and bake the gizzards until they are easily pierced with a fork, about 2 hours. Let the gizzards cool to room temperature in the fat. (If not using right away, pack the gizzards into a container, cover with the fat, cover, and refrigerate for up to 3 weeks.)

Remove the gizzards from the dish, scraping away any clinging fat. In a frying pan, cook the gizzards over medium heat just until warmed through, about 5 minutes. Keep warm.

In a salad bowl, whisk together the oil and vinegar, then whisk in the shallot and the remaining ½ teaspoon salt and ¼ teaspoon pepper. Add the greens and half of the chives and toss to coat. Divide the greens among 4 salad plates and top with the gizzards. Chop half of the hazelnuts and scatter over the salads with the remaining whole nuts and chives. Serve at once.

SERVES 4

1 lb (500 g) chicken gizzards

1 tsp juniper berries, crushed

1½ tsp sea salt

¾ tsp freshly ground pepper

1 clove garlic, minced

1–1½ cups (7–11 oz/220–345 g) duck fat or lard

3 Tbsp hazelnut oil

1½ Tbsp sherry vinegar

1 Tbsp minced shallot

2 cups (2 oz/60 g) wild young dandelion greens or coarsely chopped baby spinach

1 cup (1 oz/30 g) wild or baby arugula

½ head butter lettuce, torn into bite-size pieces

10 fresh chives, cut into 1-inch (2.5-cm) lengths

¼ cup (1¼ oz/35 g) hazelnuts, toasted

CHERRY CHUTNEY with DUCK BREAST

Cherries are among the first fruits to ripen, starting in late April and going into early July. Most varieties are sweet, such as Bing and Jubilee. Fresh sour cherries are difficult to find, even at farmers' markets, which is a good case for growing your own. This quick chutney uses the readily available sweet cherries, but sour cherries also make an excellent chutney if you add a little more honey.

To make the chutney, measure ¼ cup (1½ oz/45 g) of the cherries, cut them in half, and set aside. In a saucepan, heat the oil over medium-high heat. Add the onion and celery and sauté until the onion is nearly translucent, about 2 minutes. Add the remaining cherries, the vinegar, and ginger, reduce the heat to medium, and cook, stirring and pressing against the cherries, until slightly thickened, 4–5 minutes. Stir in the honey and salt and continue to cook, stirring, until the mixture thickens and the onion, celery, and cherries are soft, 3–4 minutes. Let cool slightly, then taste and adjust the seasoning. Set aside.

To prepare the duck, using a sharp knife, cut through the skin and into the fat (but not the meat) in a crosshatch pattern, allowing about ½ inch (12 mm) between the cuts. Pat the duck dry and sprinkle all over with the salt and pepper.

Smear the butter in a frying pan, place the duck breasts, skin side down, in the pan, and place over medium heat. Cook until the skin is crisp and golden, 7–8 minutes. Flip the breasts and cook, brushing the crispy skin with the honey, until the second side is browned and the meat is cooked to medium-rare to medium (135°–140°F/57°–60°C on an instant-read thermometer), 4–6 minutes. Using tongs, turn the breasts, one at a time, to sear each side until browned, about 1 minute per side.

Transfer to a carving board and let stand for 5 minutes. Meanwhile, reheat the chutney over low heat, stirring, until warmed through. Stir in the reserved cherries.

Carve the duck into ½-inch (12-mm) slices, reserving any juices. Arrange on 4 warmed dinner plates or on a platter, drizzle with the juices, and accompany with the chutney.

SERVES 4

for the chutney

1 lb (500 g) cherries, pitted (about 2 cups/ 11 oz/345 g)

1 Tbsp grapeseed or canola oil

¼ cup (1¼ oz/35 g) chopped yellow onion

¼ cup (1½ oz/45 g) finely chopped celery

1 Tbsp sherry vinegar

1-inch (2.5-cm) piece fresh ginger, peeled and grated (about 1 tsp)

1 Tbsp honey

¼ tsp sea salt

for the duck

2 skin-on duck breasts, 2–2½ lb (1–1.25 kg) total, at room temperature for 30 minutes

½ tsp sea salt

½ tsp freshly ground pepper

1 Tbsp unsalted butter, at room temperature

1 Tbsp honey

FIG-GLAZED & FIG-STUFFED PORK RIB ROAST

Figs are one of the most glorious late-summer and fall fruits, and the trees are among the most hardy fruit trees to grow in a home orchard, as they are impervious to most disease and seem to thrive with a minimum of fuss. Ripe figs are relatively fragile and don't ship well, which means we frequently see underripe, flavorless fruits in markets. With a fig tree in your yard, you can pick the fruit when it's perfectly ripe and bring it directly into your kitchen. Since fresh figs lose a bit of their intense flavor when cooked, I combine them with dried figs for a stuffing or a sauce, as I do here, to ensure the fig flavor is manifest. This special-occasion dish calls for a bone-in pork loin roast and has both a glaze and a pan sauce.

To prepare the pork, preheat the oven to 475°F (245°C). Use a sharp knife to separate the rib bones from the roast, keeping the knife as close to the bones as possible as you cut them away. (Or ask your butcher to separate the bones from the roast and to tie them back on with string for the trip home. Then, just before seasoning and stuffing the roast, snip the string holding the bones in place.)

Trim the stems from 4 of the fresh figs and all of the dried figs. Chop these figs and put them in a small bowl with the brandy, ½ teaspoon of the salt, ¼ teaspoon of the pepper, the sage, pepper flakes, and garlic. Let stand until you can mash the mixture with the back of the fork to make a paste, about 15 minutes. (Dried figs can take some time to soften up.)

Rub the meat and bones all over with the remaining ½ teaspoon salt and ¼ teaspoon pepper. With the bone side of the meat facing up, pack it with the fig stuffing. Place the ribs back in place, making sure they are in the same direction as they were cut, and tie them on with several pieces of kitchen string. It may be easier to do this if you have someone to help you.

continued on next page

SERVES 4–6

for the pork

3 lb (1.5 kg) bone-in
pork loin roast,
about 4 ribs

7 ripe fresh figs,
any variety

4 dried figs, any variety

2 Tbsp brandy

1 tsp coarse sea salt

½ tsp freshly
ground pepper

½ tsp dried sage

¼ tsp red
pepper flakes

1 clove garlic, minced

➡

To make the glaze, combine ½ cup (4 fl oz/125 ml) water, the wine, dried figs, honey, and sage in a saucepan. Bring to a boil over medium-high heat, then reduce the heat to medium and simmer until the figs are soft and the glaze is reduced to about ½ cup (4 fl oz/125 ml). Remove from the heat and strain the glaze through a chinois or fine-mesh sieve, pressing on the figs with the back of a spoon. Discard the solids.

Place the stuffed roast, bone side down, in an ovenproof frying pan and roast for 15 minutes. Reduce the heat to 325°F (165°F). Baste for the first time with the glaze and continue to roast, basting several more times with the glaze, until an instant-read thermometer inserted into the meat but not touching the bone registers 140°–145°F (60°–63°C) on an instant-read thermometer, about 45 minutes. Transfer the roast to a carving board, cover loosely with aluminum foil, and let rest for 5–10 minutes before carving.

While the roast is resting, slice the remaining 3 fresh figs and set aside.

To carve the roast, snip the strings and gently remove the ribs. Carve the roast into ¼-inch (6-mm) or ½-inch (12-mm) slices (depending on your preference), reserving any juices. Arrange the pork slices on a platter. Slice between the ribs to separate them and arrange them on the platter, too. Cover loosely with foil while you prepare a pan sauce.

To prepare the pan sauce, pour the collected juices from the carving board into a saucepan along with any succulent bits from the frying pan (don't include any burnt bits). Add the wine and bring to a boil over high heat. Stir in the butter and continue to cook until reduced by about half. Drizzle the pan sauce over the sliced pork and garnish with the reserved fresh fig slices. Serve at once.

for the glaze

½ cup (4 fl oz/125 ml) dry red wine such as Merlot or Pinot Noir

3 dried figs, any variety, stemmed and finely chopped

1 tsp honey

½ tsp dried sage

for the pan sauce

2 Tbsp dry red wine such as Merlot or Pinot Noir

1 Tbsp unsalted butter

MULBERRY & PISTACHIO TART

Mulberry trees are closely associated with the French silk industry. Thousands of trees were planted to succor the worms that eat the leaves and spin silk threads. The silk industry declined in the 1800s, but the mulberry trees remain. In Provence, they are pruned each winter to force the long branches, which are attached to lateral wires, to provide a dense shade canopy. Many homes and restaurants have them planted just for this reason. The small, elongated berry-like fruits can be purple, pink, or white, and sweetness varies. Their season is short, and any fresh berries can be substituted here. The pistachios add both crunch and color to the shortbread crust. I suggest purchasing the nuts in the shell, as they tend to retain their texture better than shelled nuts.

Preheat the oven to 350°F (180°C).

To make the pastry, shell the pistachios. You should have about ½ cup (2 oz/60 g). Use a mortar and pestle, clean coffee grinder, or small food processor to grind together the pistachios and 2 tablespoons of the sugar until the nuts are coarsely ground. You may need to work in batches. Some of the pistachios will be finely ground, others chunkier. Set aside.

In a bowl, stir together the flour and the remaining ¼ cup (2 oz/60 g) sugar. Add the butter and work it in with your fingers or a pastry cutter until crumbly and the size of peas. Add the egg and mix it with a fork. Tightly pack the dough into a ball. Using your fingers, press the dough evenly into the bottom and up the sides of a 9-inch (23-cm) fluted tart pan with a removable bottom. Sprinkle half of the pistachio-sugar mixture over the pastry and gently press it in.

Bake until the crust turns lightly golden and pulls away slightly from the sides of the pan, 15–20 minutes. Set aside to cool.

To make the pastry cream, in a saucepan, heat the milk over medium-high heat just until fine bubbles form around the edges, about 2 minutes. Do not boil.

continued on next page

SERVES 6–8

for the pastry
1 cup (4 oz/125 g) pistachios in the shell

¼ cup (2 oz/60 g) plus 2 Tbsp sugar

1½ cups (7½ oz/235 g) all-purpose flour

4 Tbsp (2 oz/60 g) cold unsalted butter, cut into ½-inch (12-mm) chunks

1 large egg

for the pastry cream
1 cup (8 fl oz/250 ml) whole milk, plus milk as needed

½ cup (4 oz/125 g) sugar

3 large egg yolks

⅓ cup (2 oz/60 g) all-purpose flour

1 Tbsp unsalted butter, at room temperature

1-inch (2.5-cm) piece vanilla bean, split lengthwise

➡

In a bowl, using an electric beater, beat together the sugar and egg yolks until the mixture is a light lemon color, about 2 minutes. Beat in the flour to form a thick paste, about 1 minute longer.

Gradually pour the hot milk into the sugar mixture, beating continuously. When the milk has been thoroughly incorporated, pour the mixture back into the saucepan, bring to a boil over medium-high heat, and cook, beating continuously, until the mixture thickens, 1–2 minutes. Immediately remove from the heat and whisk vigorously until very thick, about 1 minute. Whisk in the butter and scrape the vanilla seeds into the pastry cream.

Let cool slightly. If the pastry cream seems too thick to spread, add up to 1 tablespoon more milk. Pour the pastry cream evenly into the pastry shell, smoothing the top.

To prepare the berry topping, in a large bowl, gently toss together the mulberries, sugar, and lemon juice. If serving the tart with whipped cream, set aside about 16 mulberries for garnishing the cream.

Lay the mulberries on the pastry cream, heaping them a bit in the middle. Sprinkle with the remaining pistachio-sugar mixture. (If not serving right away, cover loosely with plastic wrap or aluminum foil and refrigerate. Let stand at room temperature for 10–15 minutes before serving.)

Slip a knife around the edges of the pan to loosen any clinging bits of pastry. Gently push on the bottom of the pan, nudging the ring loose. Slide the tart onto a serving plate.

If serving the tart with whipped cream, pour the cream into a bowl and, using the electric beater, whip the cream until it starts to thicken. Add the sugar and continue to beat until stiff peaks form.

Cut the tart into wedges. Top each serving with a dollop of whipped cream, if using, and top the cream with a mulberry or two. Serve at once.

for the berry topping

3 cups (14 oz/430 g) fresh mulberries

1½ Tbsp sugar

Juice of 1 lemon

for the whipped cream (optional)

½ cup (4 fl oz/125 ml) heavy cream

1 Tbsp sugar

OVEN-ROASTED OR GRILLED FRUITS

My favorite way to make this simple dessert is in my outdoor wood-fired oven, after the pizzas have come out or the sardines or chickens have finished roasting. The oven is still hot, but not too hot, and it gives the fruit a slightly smoky overtone. However, I've made the same dish many times in my kitchen oven and on my wood-fired grill. You can compose your own version of this dish whenever your local fruits begin to ripen, from late spring until fall. Choose a selection of apricots, plums, peaches, nectarines, figs, or even grapes, depending on the season.

If oven roasting, halve the stone fruits, leave the figs whole, and halve or leave the grapes whole, or both. Arrange the fruits in a baking dish, sprinkle them with extra-virgin olive oil and sugar, toss to coat, and then roast at 475°F (245°C) until soft, lightly golden, and some juices begin to run, about 15 minutes. If grilling, halve the stone fruits and figs and divide the grapes into clusters, then coat lightly with olive oil and a touch of sugar. Prepare a charcoal or wood fire in a grill or preheat a gas grill. Rub the grill grates with olive oil. When the grill is hot, place the fruits, cut side down, on the grate and grill, turning once, until juicy and etched with grill marks. The timing depends on the type and ripeness of the fruit. These warm fruits are especially good topped with vanilla ice cream, which gradually pools into a kind of crème anglaise.

BLOOD ORANGE RUSTIC TART

Even though citrus is grown in only a small area along the French Mediterranean coast, so much citrus is grown throughout the Mediterranean Basin that the fruits are a winter staple in France. Blood oranges are eaten on their own or used in cooking, and the peels are often dried for seasoning. Fruit tarts are a common homemade dessert, and this is one of the easiest I know.

Preheat the oven to 375°F (190°C). Line a rimmed baking sheet with parchment paper.

On a floured work surface, roll the puff pastry into a rough rectangle a scant ½ inch (12 mm) thick. Carefully transfer the puff pastry to the prepared baking sheet. Gather the edges up and fold them over on themselves to form a generous ½-inch (12-mm) rim. Freeze the pastry on the baking sheet for 15 minutes or refrigerate for 1 hour to firm up the edges.

Cut the unpeeled oranges crosswise into ½-inch (12-mm) slices. With the knife, trim the peels, and then with the tip of the knife, remove the seeds.

Remove the pastry from the freezer. Arrange the oranges snugly in a single layer on the chilled pastry and sprinkle with the ½ cup (4 oz/125 g) sugar.

Bake until the pastry is puffed and browned and the oranges have caramelized slightly, about 30 minutes. Cover loosely with aluminum foil and let cool for 10 minutes.

To make a topping, if you like, stir together the crème fraîche and the remaining 2 tablespoons sugar in a small bowl.

Cut the tart into rectangles. Serve warm with dollops of sweetened crème fraîche, if using.

SERVES 6-8

1 sheet frozen puff pastry (about ½ lb/250 g), thawed

3–4 blood oranges or a mix of blood oranges and navel oranges

½ cup (4 oz/125 g) sugar, plus 2 Tbsp (optional)

1 cup (8 fl oz/250 ml) crème fraîche (optional)

FIG & HONEY SOUFFLÉ

The figs give this soufflé an unusual, light bisque color with just a hint of mauve. I like to serve it plain, but it could be given a light dusting of confectioners' sugar just before serving.

Preheat the oven to 400°F (200°C).

Trim the stems from the fresh and dried figs. Chop 4 of the fresh figs into 5 or 6 pieces each and set aside. Slice the remaining 2 fresh figs lengthwise and reserve for garnish.

Combine 1 cup (8 fl oz/250 ml) water, the dried figs, and honey in a saucepan and bring to a boil over medium heat. Reduce the heat to low and simmer until the figs are soft and have soaked up some of the liquid, about 15 minutes. Drain the figs, reserving the cooking liquid, and then chop them.

Using a blender, purée the fresh and dried figs until they have a jam-like consistency, adding a tablespoon or so of the cooking liquid if necessary. The fig mixture should not be runny. Strain the purée through a chinois or fine-mesh sieve, pressing on the solids with the back of a spoon. Discard the solids. You should have about ½ cup (4 fl oz/125 ml) strained fig purée. Set aside.

Rub the inside of a 6-cup (48–fl oz/1.5-l) soufflé mold with the butter. Add 3 tablespoons of the sugar and tip the mold to coat the bottom and sides thoroughly. This will help the soufflé to rise and ensure a sugary crust. Turn the mold upside down and gently tap to remove any excess sugar.

In a large bowl, using an electric beater, whip the egg whites with ⅛ teaspoon of the salt until soft peaks form. Turn off the beater, sprinkle with 1 tablespoon of the sugar, and then continue to beat until stiff peaks form. Set aside.

SERVES 4

6 large fresh figs, any variety

3 dried figs, any variety

2 Tbsp honey

2 tsp unsalted butter

⅓ cup (3 oz/90 g) plus 4 Tbsp (2 oz/60 g) sugar

5 large egg whites plus 4 large egg yolks

¼ tsp sea salt

¾ cup (6 fl oz/180 ml) whole milk

3 Tbsp cornstarch

In a saucepan over medium-high heat, mix together a few tablespoons of the milk and the cornstarch until a thick paste forms. Add the remaining ⅛ teaspoon salt and then slowly pour in the remaining milk, whisking constantly. Then add the remaining ⅓ cup (3 oz/90 g) sugar, continuing to whisk until a thick sauce forms, about 1 minute. Remove from the heat and spoon in 1 egg yolk, whisking it into the sauce until combined. Whisk in the remaining 3 egg yolks, one at a time, until combined. Stir in the fig purée.

Gently stir in about one-quarter of the stiff egg whites. Then, using a rubber spatula, carefully fold in the remaining egg whites, one-quarter at a time. Err on the side of less folding, as it's better if the soufflé batter has some streaks of unincorporated egg white than if it is folded too long and the air lost, which can result in a deflated soufflé.

Still using the spatula, spoon the soufflé mixture into the prepared mold and then smooth the top. The mixture should reach to within 1¼ inches (3 cm) of the rim of the mold.

Place the mold in the oven and immediately reduce the heat to 375°F (190°C). Bake until a long, thin skewer inserted horizontally through the puffed crown comes out clean, 30–35 minutes.

Garnish with the reserved sliced fresh figs and serve at once.

WALNUT & ALMOND TART

Walnuts and almonds feature in many French dishes, from pastries to fortified wines, and are grown in various regions of the country, where they can be seen in home orchards as well as in large commercial plantings. In Provence, they are meant to be two of the thirteen desserts at the traditional Christmas Eve table (page 126), either on their own or as part of a confection, such as in this nut tart. If you like, serve wedges of the tart with vanilla, caramel, or Winter Savory Ice Cream (page 228).

Preheat the oven to 350°F (180°C).

To make the pastry, in a bowl, stir together the flour and granulated sugar. Add the butter and work it in with your fingers or a pastry cutter until crumbly and the size of peas. Add the egg and mix it with a fork. Tightly pack the dough into a ball. Using your fingers, press the dough evenly onto the bottom and up the sides of a 9-inch (23-cm) fluted tart pan with a removable bottom. Set aside.

To make the filling, in a bowl, combine the brown sugar, eggs, and melted butter. Split the vanilla bean lengthwise and scrape the seeds into the bowl. Whisk until well blended. Stir in the nuts, then pour the filling evenly into the tart shell, smoothing the top with a spatula. The filling should reach to within ¼ inch (6 mm) of the rim of the tart pan.

Bake until the crust and filling are golden brown, about 50 minutes. Transfer to a rack to cool to room temperature. Slip a knife around the edges of the pan to loosen any clinging bits of pastry. Gently push on the bottom of the pan, nudging the ring loose. Slide the tart onto a serving plate, cut into wedges, and serve.

SERVES 8

for the pastry

1½ cups (7½ oz/235 g) all-purpose flour

¼ cup (2 oz/60 g) granulated sugar

4 Tbsp (2 oz/60 g) cold unsalted butter, cut into ½-inch (12-mm) chunks

1 large egg

for the filling

½ cup (3½ oz/105 g) firmly packed golden brown sugar

2 large eggs

2 Tbsp unsalted butter, melted and cooled

1-inch (2.5-cm) piece vanilla bean

¾ cup (3 oz/90 g) walnuts, coarsely chopped and lightly toasted

¾ cup (4 oz/125 g) almonds, coarsely chopped and lightly toasted

CHESTNUT CREAM PROFITEROLES

Profiteroles are one of the sweets most associated with France. While they are easy to make at home, they are also often available at pâtisseries. The smooth chestnut cream filling and the chocolate glaze that I have used here make an exceptional combination.

Preheat the oven to 425°F (220°C). Place racks in the upper and lower thirds of the oven. Line 2 baking sheets with parchment paper.

In a saucepan, combine 1 cup (8 fl oz/250 ml) water, the butter, and salt. Bring to a boil over medium-high heat and cook, stirring, until the butter melts, 3–4 minutes. Add the flour all at once and stir vigorously with a wooden spoon until a thick paste forms and pulls away from the sides of the pan, about 3 minutes. Remove from the heat and make a well in the center of the paste. Add the eggs, one at a time, to the well, beating after each addition. You should have a smooth, sticky batter.

Have ready a glass of hot water and a metal tablespoon. To shape each puff, dip the spoon into the water, scoop up a generous spoonful of the dough, and push it onto a prepared baking sheet. Repeat, spacing the puffs 2 inches (5 cm) apart and dipping the spoon each time. Lightly brush the puffs with the egg wash, being careful not to drip onto the pan.

Bake for 10 minutes, then reduce the heat to 350°F (180°C) and continue to bake until the pastries are golden brown and crunchy, about 15 minutes longer. When done, pierce the side of each pastry with a skewer, turn off the oven, and leave in the oven for 15 minutes to dry. Remove from the oven and cut in half horizontally.

While the pastries are baking, make the glaze: In a bowl, whisk together the confectioners' sugar and cocoa powder. Stir in the milk until a spreadable paste forms, adding more milk, a few drops at a time, if needed. Spread each warm profiterole top with a little of the glaze. (At this point, the pastries can be set aside for up to 6 hours until ready to fill and serve.)

To assemble, place the profiterole bottoms on a platter. Spoon a tablespoonful of the chestnut cream onto each bottom and finish with a glazed top. Serve at once.

MAKES ABOUT
30 PROFITEROLES

6 Tbsp (3½ oz/105 g)
unsalted butter

½ tsp sea salt

1¼ cups (6½ oz/200 g)
all-purpose flour

4 large eggs

Boiling water for
dipping spoon

1 large egg beaten
with 1 Tbsp water
for egg wash

for the glaze

2 cups (8 oz/250 g)
confectioners' sugar

¼ cup (¾ oz/20 g)
unsweetened
cocoa powder

2 Tbsp whole milk,
plus up to 1 Tbsp
more if needed

¾ lb (375 g) purchased
sweetened chestnut
spread *(crème
de marrons)*

THE THIRTEEN DESSERTS OF CHRISTMAS IN PROVENCE

Tradition says that Provence's thirteen desserts of Christmas are symbolic of the Last Supper, when Christ last dined with his twelve apostles. Almonds, walnuts, figs, and raisins are called the *quatre mendiants*, or "four beggars," because the colors of the nuts and fruits symbolize the monks' robes of the four religious orders that are vowed to poverty: almonds for the Carmelites, walnuts for the Augustinians, figs for the Franciscans, and raisins for the Dominicans. As time has passed, the religious significance of the thirteen desserts has waned, but the cultural importance endures.

In old Provence, the table for *le gros souper*, or Christmas Eve dinner, was set with three white tablecloths, representing the Holy Trinity, and decorated with three shallow dishes of sprouted wheat seed that had been planted on December 4, the Feast of Saint Barbara. The wheat seed symbolized the promise of a good harvest for the coming year. Bottles of sweet *vin cuit*, a dessert wine made with grape must, were also on the table, along with pinecones and moss gathered from the forest. A meatless meal of seven fish dishes, such as salt cod, and vegetables, such as cardoons (page 76), was served before going to mass. At midnight, after returning from mass, the desserts were served, sometimes along with a roast goose.

The exact composition of the thirteen desserts varies from village to village in Provence, with one thing in common: at least twelve of the desserts should be composed entirely of *produits de terroir* (locally grown ingredients), while the thirteenth can be something exotic, such as a date or a tangerine. Originally, all of the ingredients were the products of self-sustaining farms and made in the farm kitchen, but as time has passed, many of the products are purchased, though still made from local ingredients.

Here is a typical composition of the thirteen desserts:

Pâtisserie, often a *fougasse* made with olive oil and orange blossom water	Raisins
Sweet biscuits or cookies	Prunes or dates
White nougat	Apples
Black nougat	Oranges
Almonds	Green melons (certain varieties that are winter keepers)
Walnuts	Quince paste
Figs	

In the simplest version, the thirteen desserts were served unadorned. Bowls of dried fruits, plates of nougat and quince paste, and fresh fruits were set out on the dessert table. Today, creative versions are common in both homes and restaurants, with fresh citrus or nuts turned into tarts (such as the Walnut & Almond Tart on page 122), the figs stuffed with chocolate or nuts, and the dried fruits used in cakes.

VIN de CITRON

Anne, my French friend who gave me this recipe and guided me through the steps, is known for her aperitif parties, which always feature her house-made infused wines, as well as the usual pastis and rosé. Her vin de citron, an aperitif made with lemons and white wine and fortified with eau-de-vie, is usually the bottle that needs to be replenished first. Serve chilled or over ice.

Using a citrus zester, zest the 2 lemons in long peels. Cut 1 lemon into quarters. Reserve the other lemon for another use.

Combine the wine, eau-de-vie, sugar, vanilla bean, lemon peels, and lemon quarters in a dry, sterilized jar with a lid. Seal the jar and store in a cool, dark place for 4 days, stirring daily to dissolve the sugar.

Line a fine-mesh sieve with cheesecloth. Strain the wine, discarding the solids. Pour the wine into a dry, sterilized bottle, seal closed, and store in a cool, dark place or in the refrigerator for up to 6 months.

MAKES 1 (750-ML) BOTTLE

2 organic lemons

1 (750-ml) bottle dry or fruity white wine, such as Sauvignon Blanc

¾ cup (6 fl oz/180 ml) eau-de-vie or vodka

½ cup (4 oz/125 g) sugar

½ vanilla bean, split lengthwise

VIN d'ORANGE

This classic French farmhouse wine is simplicity itself. In France, bitter Seville oranges are most often used, but I've found that navel or blood oranges from my backyard trees turn out a perfectly delicious wine. Served chilled or over ice.

Preheat the oven to 300°F (150°C). Using a citrus zester, zest the oranges, including some pith, in long peels. Spread the peels on a baking sheet and bake, turning occasionally, until the pith is golden and the skin is dark orange, about 45 minutes.

Combine the wine, sugar, eau-de-vie, and toasted peels in a dry, sterilized jar with a lid. Seal the jar and store in a cool, dark place, turning it several times until the sugar dissolves, about 1 week. Continue to store for at least 1 month or preferably 2–3 months.

Line a fine-mesh sieve with cheesecloth and strain the wine, discarding the peels. Pour into a dry, sterilized bottle, seal closed, and store in a cool, dark place or in the refrigerator for up to 1 year.

MAKES 1 (750-ML) BOTTLE

6 small or 4 large organic oranges

1 (750-ml) bottle dry or fruity white wine, rosé, or red wine

¾ cup (6 oz/185 g) sugar

½ cup (4 fl oz/125 ml) eau-de-vie or vodka

ORCHARD IN A JAR

I like to think of *vieux garçon*, or "bachelor's brandied fruit," as the essence of a fruit orchard captured in a jar. It is a traditional country preparation in which fruit and sugar are combined with brandy or another spirit and left to macerate. Starting in June with cherries, layers of fruit are put into a crock, then covered with sugar and alcohol. As other fruits ripen throughout the summer, they are added to the crock, along with more sugar and brandy and so on, throughout the fall. When winter comes, the brandied fruits are eaten and the sweetened brandy imbibed. The origin of the name is lost in legend, though two scenarios are popular: the *vieux garçon* is easy enough for a bachelor to make, or a bachelor could drown his sorrows with the fruity liquor on the long, dark, and lonely nights of winter.

The method is simple. Rub the fruits with a kitchen towel to remove any dust. Remove any stems and pierce the fruits all over with a sterilized needle. Leave small fruits, like cherries and apricots, whole; pit and then halve or quarter larger fruits, like peaches and nectarines. For each 2 cups (4½ –5½ oz/140–170 g) of fruit, add 1 cup (8 oz/250 g) sugar. Take a widemouthed crock or glass jar with a lid—a 1-gal (3.8-l) size is good. Add the prepared fruit, one type at a time, and sprinkle with the sugar. Add vodka to cover. Weight the fruit down with a small saucer; the fruit should always be submerged. Seal the jar. As new fruits come into season, add them in the same fashion: fruit, sugar, and vodka. If the kitchen isn't too hot, the jar can sit on your kitchen counter, but it should be kept out of the sunlight. Any kind of fruit, other than citrus, can be used for *vieux garçon*. Berries will disintegrate, but do give a good flavor. Let the fruits macerate for at least 3 months before sipping a glassful of the amber-rose liquid or sampling the alcohol-infused fruit. You can strain the liquid if you desire, but it is not necessary. It will for keep up to 1 year or more in a cool, dark place.

CHAPTER THREE

THE BARNYARD

THE BARNYARD

COWS, GOATS, SHEEP, PIGS, CHICKENS, DUCKS & RABBITS

WHEN I MOVED TO RURAL FRANCE AND SAW THAT ALMOST ALL OF MY NEIGHBORS HAD SOME VERSION OF A BARNYARD, I WAS REMINDED OF THE STORYBOOKS of my childhood, where cows and pigs, chickens and rabbits shared a living space and talked to one another all day long. I was enchanted.

My neighbors, however, didn't romanticize this part of daily life. And I quickly gave up the idea of the happy, chatty barnyard as I discovered that the relationship between the animals and the table was a simple and practical one. Animals destined for the table were left unnamed, while those kept for milk, eggs, or breeding purposes were christened thoughtfully.

Rabbits were kept in hutches that were more or less waist-high. They were fed freshly cut alfalfa or other grasses, as well as a few table scraps and feed pellets. The droppings fell through the wire hutch to the ground below, where the chickens happily ate them, along with some grain, grasses, and more table scraps. Ducks, guinea hens, and geese roamed freely, eating bugs and snails. All of the animals came back to the barnyard boxes or pens at night. Foxes were serious predators, and more than a few of my neighbors lost animals to them. The rabbits and guinea hens supplied meat for the table, and the chickens and ducks gave us both eggs and meat.

Some people kept large herds of sheep and goats that were housed in ancient stone barns. The animals were taken out across the hills and valleys to roam for food and brought back at night, except during the long transhumance (page 162), when they were taken to the high mountain pastures in summer and returned home in fall. Other people kept just a few sheep and a goat or two for milk and cheese making and, eventually, for meat. Our own goat herd was small, about thirty head, and all were named, since they were for milking. We even named our young buck, since we intended to keep him for several years.

The family pig had its own space, usually a stone structure adjacent to the barnyard. Family pigs were raised to provide the preserved meats, such as sausages, hams, and pâtés that would provision the larder for a year. Our pig, however, was a breeding pig, and we named her Lucretia. M. Gos,

from whom we bought her, showed us the stone enclosure at our house that he called a *cochonerie*, and it was there she lived and had her litters, except for a walk and forage each day.

Cows were rare on a Provençal farmstead, due, no doubt, to the dry Mediterranean climate. But elsewhere in France, in wetter, greener areas, a family cow or two was an essential part of the barnyard, supplying milk for cheese and for butter, the staple fat throughout most of France, except for the south, where olive oil predominates.

The barnyard was the nexus of the sustainable life and the source of so much that bound the kitchen together, from gratins and stews to tarts and pastries, and, of course, the essential charcuterie. Even today, people who can tend to keep at least a few chickens and maybe a goat or two. There is a renaissance, too, of the old traditions, and some people are again keeping a few sheep, ducks, and a pig, not out of necessity but from a desire to raise their own food, ensuring its quality.

COCOTTE of EGGS with FRESH TOMATO & BASIL

There is nothing quite like fresh eggs, and that is where the barnyard excels. If nothing else, a few laying chickens in your backyard will connect you with your own food. The golden, almost orange yolks from a well-fed bird are singular and will transform your notion of what eggs should look and taste like. This simple egg preparation, baked in small, individual dishes, or cocottes, *is just the place to show off backyard-fresh eggs. Serve the* cocottes *as a first course or as part of a simple lunch.*

Preheat the oven to 425°F (220°C). Have ready four ½-cup (4–fl oz/125-ml) ramekins and a baking dish just large enough to hold the ramekins.

In a frying pan, heat the olive oil over medium-high heat. When it is hot, add the onion and sauté until soft, about 3 minutes. Add the tomatoes, salt, and pepper and sauté until the tomatoes begin to release their juice, about 2 minutes longer. Reduce the heat to medium and continue to cook until thickened, 3–4 minutes longer.

Stack the basil leaves on top of one another, roll up tightly, and slice thinly into chiffonade. Divide the cut basil evenly among the ramekins. Divide the tomato mixture evenly among the ramekins, then crack 1 egg into each one.

Bring a kettle of water to a boil over high heat. Cover each ramekin snugly with aluminum foil and place in the baking dish. Pour the boiling water into the baking dish until it reaches halfway up the sides of the ramekins. Bake until the whites of the eggs are just set, 8–10 minutes. Check for doneness by lifting the foil.

Remove the ramekins from the baking dish, remove the foil, and garnish with more basil. Serve at once.

SERVES 4

1 Tbsp extra-virgin olive oil

¼ cup (1½ oz/45 g) minced yellow onion

2 cups (12 oz/375 g) chopped tomatoes

½ tsp sea salt

¼ tsp freshly ground pepper

6–8 fresh basil leaves, depending on size, plus small leaves for garnish

4 large eggs

SPINACH, MUSHROOM &
HAM CREPES, GRATINÉED

Here, crepes, a staple of the French menu, are rolled around a hearty filling, tucked tightly into a baking dish, slathered with a traditional Mornay sauce, strewn with cheese, and then gratinéed until a golden crust forms, for a great brunch or supper dish, served with a salad.

To make the filling, in a frying pan, melt the butter over medium-high heat. Add the shallot and sauté until translucent, 2–3 minutes. Add the mushrooms and sauté until they are soft and have released their juices, 4–5 minutes. Add the spinach, parsley, salt, and pepper and cook until just warmed through, about 5 minutes. Taste and adjust the seasoning. Set aside.

To make the sauce, in a saucepan, melt the butter over medium-high heat. Immediately remove the pan from the heat and slowly whisk in the flour to make a roux. Return to medium-high heat and slowly drizzle in 1½ cups (12 fl oz/375 ml) of the milk, whisking thoroughly to prevent lumps. Whisk in the salt, pepper, and cayenne, reduce the heat to medium, and continue to cook, whisking from time to time, until thickened, about 15 minutes, adding more milk if the sauce becomes too thick. Whisk in ⅔ cup (2½ oz/75 g) of the cheese until melted. Set aside.

Preheat the oven to 450°F (230°C). Rub the inside of a 11-by-7-by-2-inch (28-by-18-by-5-cm) baking or gratin dish with ½ teaspoon of the butter.

Lay 1 crepe on a work surface. Spread about 1 tablespoon of the filling on the crepe, leaving a 1-inch (2.5-cm) border uncovered. Cover with 3–4 ham slivers, roll up the crepe, and place it, seam side down, in the baking dish. Repeat to fill the remaining crepes. Pour the sauce evenly over the crepes, dot with the remaining 1½ teaspoons butter, and sprinkle with the remaining cheese.

Bake until the sauce bubbles and the top is golden, 15–20 minutes. Let stand for 5 minutes, then carefully transfer to plates and serve at once.

SERVES 6–8

for the filling

1 Tbsp unsalted butter

2 Tbsp minced shallot

½ lb (250 g) mushrooms, any variety, minced

1 recipe Spinach à la Crème (page 63)

2 Tbsp minced fresh flat-leaf parsley

¼ tsp each sea salt and freshly ground pepper

for the sauce

2½ Tbsp unsalted butter

2 Tbsp all-purpose flour

1½–2 cups (12–16 fl oz/375–500 ml) whole milk

½ tsp each coarse sea salt and freshly ground black pepper

¼ tsp cayenne pepper

1 cup (4 oz/125 g) shredded Gruyère cheese

2 tsp unsalted butter

1 recipe Crepes (page 180)

¼ lb (125 g) thinly sliced deli-style ham, cut into ½-inch (12-mm) slivers

DUCK & JUNIPER CRÉPINETTES

Crépinettes are essentially sausages wrapped in caul fat (also known as lace fat), which is the fat that encases the liver of a pig. They can be made with any type of meat—pork, rabbit, duck, chicken, lamb—and the seasonings can vary as well. I especially like this version made with duck and seasoned with juniper and thyme. If you cannot find caul fat, you can still make the duck sausage and shape it into patties.

Remove the skin and trim the fat from the ducks; reserve for another use (pages 105 and 219). Remove the meat from the breast and legs and cut it into 1-inch (2.5-cm) pieces. Discard the bones. You should have about 3½ lb (1.75 kg) meat. In a bowl, combine the duck meat and the fatback.

In a small bowl, stir together the salt, juniper berries, pepper, and sage. Add the salt mixture to the meat and fatback, mixing well with your hands. Cover and refrigerate overnight.

Put the parts of your grinder into the freezer to chill for 1 hour. (If the meat mixture or the grinder is warm, the fat will melt, rather than bind.) Set up the chilled grinder according to the manufacturer's instructions and fit it with the medium grinding plate. Working in batches, grind the meat mixture and transfer to a large bowl. Mix with your hands until well combined. Fry a nugget of the mixture, taste, and adjust the seasoning of the meat mixture if needed. Preheat the oven to 375°F (190°C).

Shape the meat mixture into 3-inch (7.5-cm) patties ½ inch (12 mm) thick. Cut the caul fat into 5-inch (13-cm) squares. Lay a square over a patty, then turn them over together, tucking the edges of the fat under the patty. Repeat with the remaining meat mixture and caul fat. (If not using right away, cover and refrigerate for up to 2 days or freeze for up to 2 months.)

Place the wrapped sausage, tucked side down, on a rimmed baking sheet. Bake until the caul fat has almost dissolved and the sausage is golden brown and cooked through, about 20 minutes. Serve at once.

MAKES ABOUT
16 CREPINETTES, EACH
ABOUT 5 OZ (155 G)

2 ducks, about 5 lb
(2.5 kg) total

1½ lb (750 g) fatback,
cut into ½-inch
(12-mm) cubes

2 Tbsp sea salt

15 juniper berries,
finely chopped

1 Tbsp freshly
ground pepper

1 Tbsp minced
fresh sage

1 lb (500 g) caul fat,
rinsed and kept
in cold water

GRILLED CHEESE SANDWICHES, FRENCH STYLE

The most well-known French grilled cheese sandwich is the croque monsieur, *made with ham and Gruyère on* pain au levain, *with a béchamel sauce covering it all. My sandwich here captures the spirit of that classic, with roasted red peppers standing in for the ham and no sauce. I love béchamel, but sometimes it's nice to skip that extra step.*

Spread 1 side of each bread slice (half or whole slice, depending on bread type used) with about 1 teaspoon butter, followed by ½ teaspoon of the mustard. Divide the cheese equally among 3 slices, followed by ½ roasted red pepper on each slice. Cover with the remaining 3 bread slices, mustard side down. Butter the top of each sandwich with about 1 teaspoon butter.

Heat a dry frying pan over medium-high heat. Place the sandwiches, buttered side down, in the pan and gently press until the edges begin to turn golden, about 3 minutes. Butter the tops of the sandwiches with about 1 teaspoon butter each, then flip the sandwiches and cook, pressing gently, until the second side is golden, about 2 minutes longer. Serve at once.

SERVES 3

3 slices cut from large loaf *pain au levain* or other coarse country bread, cut in half, or 6 slices *pain de mie* (white sandwich bread)

About 4 Tbsp (2 oz/60 g) unsalted butter, at room temperature

3 tsp Dijon mustard

¼ lb (125 g) Comté, Gruyère, or Emmentaler cheese, shredded

1½ roasted red peppers in oil, drained and patted dry

RACLETTE & ACCOUTREMENTS

In the pastures of France, cows eat the lush grass and produce cream-laden milk, which is then turned into butter and cheese and preserved. Raclette is a cow's milk cheese that melts evenly and smoothly. In the old days, it was simply put near the fire in the hearth, and as the cheese melted, it was scraped onto potatoes and eaten with pickles. Today, there are electric raclette sets, with individual serving-size pieces for each person's cheese and a grill-plate covering for vegetables or even sausages. I do like these sets, but it is also fun to melt the cheese the old-fashioned way, by the fireplace or in the oven. The essential accompaniments are the potatoes on which to spread the cheese, the cornichons, and some version of pickled onions, but you can also include various salads, charcuterie, or vegetables for grilling.

Put the potatoes in a saucepan, add the salt and water to cover by 2 inches (5 cm), and bring to a boil over medium-high heat. Reduce the heat to medium, cover, and cook until the potatoes are easily pierced with the tines of a fork, about 20 minutes. Drain the potatoes, then return them to the hot pan to keep warm.

To cook on the hearth, build a wood fire in the fireplace according to your usual method. When the fire is roaring, place a ½-lb (250-g) wedge of the raclette on a plate near the heat. As the face of the cheese closest to the fire melts, scrape some melted cheese onto 4 plates, continuously scraping and adding more cheese as it continues to melt. Repeat with the remaining cheese.

To cook in the oven, preheat the oven to 400°F (200°C). Remove any rind from the cheese and cut the cheese into ½-inch (12-mm) slices. Place 3 slices on each of 4 ovenproof plates and place them in the oven until they melt into a soft pool, 6–7 minutes.

Serve at once with the potatoes, cornichons, pickled onions, and prosciutto and allow the diners to help themselves.

SERVES 4

12 small potatoes
such as Yukon gold
or red rose

1 tsp sea salt

1 lb (500 g) raclette cheese

24 cornichons

24 small pickled onions

12 thin slices prosciutto

LAYERED QUICHE with
JAMBON CRU & BLUE CHEESE

*Eggs, milk or cream, butter, and cheese —all basic ingredients from the barnyard —
have been combined in numerous ways to create some of France's most iconic dishes.
Soufflés, quiches, and flans, in particular, serve as the basis for all kinds of
inspired combinations. This layered quiche is a favorite in my house. I like to
serve it for dinner, with the leftovers, slightly warmed, for breakfast the next day.*

Preheat the oven to 400°F (200°C). On a floured work surface, roll out the pastry dough into an 11-inch (28-cm) circle. Drape it over a 10-inch (25-cm) straight-sided quiche pan, preferably with a removable bottom, and gently press it into the pan, letting the edges hang over the sides. Tuck the excess dough under to make a folded rim.

Line the pastry with aluminum foil and add pie weights or dried beans. Bake until the exposed edges begin to turn golden, about 7 minutes. Remove the weights and foil. Prick the bottom of the pastry with a fork and bake until the crust turns a pale bisque, 2–3 minutes. Let the crust cool slightly.

Layer half of the *jambon cru* evenly in the pastry shell. Dot with ½ teaspoon dollops of half of the blue cheese. In a large bowl, whisk together the cream, whole eggs, egg yolks, and pepper. Pour about half of the cream mixture over the *jambon cru*. Coarsely chop the remaining *jambon cru* and sprinkle it over the cream mixture, followed by dollops of the remaining cheese. Pour the remaining cream mixture over the top and dot with the butter.

Bake until the top is golden and puffed and a toothpick inserted into the center comes out clean, about 25 minutes. Remove from the oven and let stand for at least 20 minutes to allow the filling to fully set before cutting. If using a pan with a removable bottom, slip a knife around the edges of the pan to loosen any clinging bits of pastry, then gently push on the bottom, nudging the ring loose. Slide the quiche onto a serving plate. Cut into wedges and serve warm or at room temperature.

SERVES 6

1 recipe lard pastry (page 183) or purchased pie dough for one 9-inch (23-cm) pie

8 thin slices jambon cru or prosciutto, each about 6 by 2 inches (15 by 5 cm)

3–4 oz (90–125 g) soft blue cheese such as bleu d'Auvergne

1½ cups (12 fl oz/375 ml) heavy cream

3 large eggs plus 2 large egg yolks

½ tsp freshly ground pepper

1 Tbsp unsalted butter

RABBIT TERRINE

Rabbits, with their ability to reproduce and mature quickly, are a fundamental part of the French barnyard, and they have a long history at the French country table. Rabbit meat is adaptable to just about any kind of cooking, from turning on a spit over an open fire to a slow braise in the oven. It's also an important element in the traditional charcuterie repertoire. Terrine de lapin is a specialty of my neighbor Robert, and he taught me to make it. The terrine can be served as a robust first course or as part of a mixed charcuterie platter with cornichons and radishes. You can cut the rabbit meat off the bones yourself, or you can ask your butcher to do so, leaving the meat in fillets and chunks as large as possible.

Slice the fatback into 9 strips, each about ¼ inch (6 mm) thick and ½ inch (12 mm) wide. Crush 12 of the juniper berries and grind the remaining 12 juniper berries with a spice grinder or clean coffee grinder. Set aside.

In a large bowl, combine ¼ cup (2 fl oz/60 ml) of the Cognac, the crushed juniper berries, the thyme, bay leaf, salt, and pepper in a large bowl. Add the rabbit meat and fatback strips and turn several times to coat. Cover and refrigerate overnight.

Preheat the oven to 350°F (180°C). Have ready a 5-cup (40–fl oz/1.25-l) terrine with a lid or a 5-cup (40–fl oz/1.25-l) loaf pan lined with aluminum foil. Also have ready a baking dish or roasting pan with 3-inch (7.5-cm) sides just large enough to hold the terrine or loaf pan.

Remove the rabbit meat and fatback from the marinade and set aside. Discard the marinade. In a bowl, using your hands, mix together the sausage and egg.

Pack one-third of the sausage mixture into the terrine or lined loaf pan. Top with one-fourth of the rabbit meat, then lay 3 fatback strips along the length of the terrine. Sprinkle with a bit of the ground juniper berries and 1 teaspoon of the Cognac. Arrange the pistachios in 2 rows down the center of the terrine, about 1½ inches (4 cm) apart, and lay the rabbit livers, if

continued on next page

SERVES 8–10

⅓ lb (5 oz/155 g) fatback

24 juniper berries

¼ cup (2 fl oz/60ml) plus 1 Tbsp Cognac

4 fresh thyme sprigs

1 dried bay leaf

1 tsp sea salt

1 tsp freshly ground pepper

2 rabbits, about 2 lb (1 kg) each, boned, with livers (if available) and bones reserved

1 lb (500 g) bulk pork sausage

1 large egg

½ cup (2 oz/60 g) pistachios in the shell, shelled

using, between them. Repeat the layering two more times, with the sausage, rabbit, fatback, ground juniper berries, and Cognac (leaving out the livers and pistachios), ending with a final layer of rabbit. Lay some of the rabbit bones across the top—I find that the small foreleg bones fit nicely—which will help the terrine to jell.

Bring a kettle of water to a boil over high heat. Cover the terrine, making sure the lid fits snugly (if you are using a loaf pan, cover it tightly with aluminum foil). Place the terrine in the baking dish. Pour the boiling water into the baking dish to reach halfway up the sides of the terrine. Bake until the rabbit meat is opaque, firm, and cooked through, 1½–2 hours.

Remove from the oven and, while still hot, uncover the terrine and remove and discard the bones. Cut a piece of aluminum foil slightly larger than the surface of the terrine and place it on top of the cooked meat, pressing it down and into the corners to make a snug fit. Wrap a brick or other item of similar weight with foil and place it on top. Refrigerate the weighted terrine for 12–24 hours.

To serve the terrine, remove the brick and foil. Heat a paring knife under running hot water, wipe dry, and run the hot knife along the edges of the terrine to loosen it. If possible, use a flexible icing spatula to loosen the bottom. If you like, serve directly from the terrine. To unmold the terrine, invert a platter on top of the mold and, holding the mold and platter, invert them together. Lift off the mold and release the terrine. If the terrine does not come free, repeat the loosening process and try again, or place the base of the mold in very hot water for 5 minutes.

Cut into 1-inch (2.5-cm) slices. Serve cold.

THE IMPORTANCE OF AN ALFALFA PATCH

Every year, my neighbor Marie planted a small alfalfa patch, only about 20 square feet (2 sq m). Each day, spring through fall, she'd go out in the late afternoon with her sickle and cut an apronful of alfalfa to feed to her rabbits. Not only was it a treat for the animals, but it also established a rhythm to the days that I admired. It was such a practical and direct thing to do: seed the alfalfa, and then when it has grown to a good height, cut some and take it to the rabbits. Chickens, goats, and sheep like alfalfa, too. Alfalfa, when watered, will continue to grow and give up to six or seven cuttings per season, except in areas with long, cold winters.

CHICKEN LIVER PÂTÉ

Also called chicken liver mousse, this is the simplest of all pâtés to make, and its smooth, creamy texture is quite different from country-style pâtés, which tend to be made with coarsely ground meats. I like to serve it as part of a big spread at a party, or as a first course in individual ramekins, accompanied by grilled toasts and pickles, or honey and salted almonds. Cherry Chutney (page 106) is also a delicious accompaniment.

Remove any fatty pieces and dark veins from the chicken livers. Rinse the livers and pat them dry, placing them on a paper towel–lined plate.

In a large frying pan, melt 3 tablespoons of the butter over medium-high heat. When it foams, add the livers and sprinkle them with the salt, pepper, and nutmeg. Reduce the heat to medium and sauté, turning frequently, until the livers are firm to the touch and still have a faint rose hue when cut open, about 12 minutes. Be careful not to overcook them. Raise the heat to medium-high, pour in the Cognac, and light it with a match or igniter. Shake the pan until the flames dissipate, scraping up any bits that cling to the bottom with a spoon, then continue to cook for about 30 seconds longer. Put the livers and pan juices in a bowl and set aside.

In the same pan, melt 3 tablespoons of the butter over medium-high heat. When it foams, add the shallot and thyme. Reduce the heat to medium and gently sauté until the shallot is very soft, about 8 minutes. Add the shallot and pan juices to the livers and let cool to room temperature.

Place the chicken liver mixture and its collected juices, the remaining ½ cup (4 oz/125 g) butter, and the cream in a food processor and process until smooth, about 3 minutes.

Using a spatula, pack the pâté into three 1-cup (8–fl oz/250-ml) ramekins or six ½ cup (4–fl oz/125-ml) ramekins or crocks, smoothing the tops. Cover with plastic wrap and refrigerate for at least 12 hours, or up to 24 hours.

Just before serving, sprinkle with the pink pepper, if desired.

SERVES 6 AS A
FIRST COURSE

1 lb (500 g) chicken livers

6 Tbsp (3 oz/90 g) unsalted butter, plus ½ cup (4 oz/125 g), cut into 1-inch (2.5-cm) chunks, at room temperature

½ tsp sea salt

½ tsp freshly ground white pepper

¼ tsp freshly grated nutmeg

3 Tbsp Cognac, Armagnac, or other brandy

1 shallot, minced

1 tsp chopped fresh thyme

5 Tbsp (3 fl oz/80 ml) heavy cream

3 Tbsp freshly ground pink peppercorns (optional)

EASY RILLETTES

Rillettes, a type of potted meat spread, always seemed esoteric to me, until my French friend Anne served me some she had made one evening at aperitif time. She explained that she just takes bits of leftover meat and cooks them with some fat and seasonings, which is a pretty good explanation of the dish. They can be made with nearly any meat or fowl and are ideally served with toasts and cornichons or assorted pickles (page 19).

(page 19)

In a large bowl, stir together the brandy, garlic, salt, pepper, and juniper berries. Add the pork shoulder and turn to coat. Cover and refrigerate overnight, or up to 48 hours.

When ready to cook, preheat the oven to 250°F (120°F).

In a large, ovenproof, heavy-bottomed saucepan, combine the fatback and ¼ cup (2 fl oz/60 ml) water and cook over low heat, stirring occasionally, until almost all of the fat has melted, about 15 minutes. Add the pork shoulder (discard the marinade) and cook until the meat shrinks slightly, releases some of its juice, and is covered in the melted fatback, about 15 minutes. Cover and bake for 1½ hours. Add the wine, re-cover the pan, and cook until the meat easily shreds with a fork, about 2 hours longer.

Place a fine-mesh sieve over a bowl and drain the pork, reserving the juices and fat in the bowl. Transfer the pork to a platter and shred it with 2 forks. As the juices and fat cool, they will separate. Pour off the fat into a small bowl and reserve it.

In a saucepan, bring the meat juices to a simmer over medium heat. Add the shredded pork, stirring to mix well; it will be a bit stiff. Gradually add 2–4 tablespoons of the reserved fat to make the mixture spreadable. Remove from the heat but keep stirring as the mixture cools to distribute the fat. Let the pork mixture cool to room temperature. Spoon the cooled mixture into a 3-cup (24–fl oz/750-ml) terrine or bowl, tap the container on a countertop to settle the contents, and smooth the top. Pour some of the reserved fat over the surface to seal. Cover and refrigerate for up to 10 days. Let stand at room temperature for 10 minutes before serving.

SERVES 6 AS A
FIRST COURSE

¼ cup (2 fl oz/60 ml) brandy

8 cloves garlic, crushed

1½ tsp sea salt

1 tsp freshly ground pepper

3 juniper berries, crushed

1 lb (500 g) boneless pork shoulder or butt, cut into ½-inch (12-mm) pieces

⅓ lb (5 oz/155 g) fatback, cut into 1-inch (2.5-cm) pieces

¼ cup (2 fl oz/60 ml) dry white wine

SHREDDED DUCK CONFIT & CORNICHON SANDWICHES

Duck leg confit is easy to make, stores well (in the refrigerator or freezer), and has many uses. Here, it is seared, warmed through, and then shredded and combined with cornichons in a sandwich. But the legs can also be served whole as a main dish, accompanied with potatoes or other vegetables, or boned and the meat and crispy skin added to salads (cut the skin into pieces). It is an essential ingredient in a traditional French cassoulet (page 157) and can be purchased if you want to skip making your own.

To prepare the duck confit, put the duck legs in a single layer in a baking dish. Combine the salt, garlic, thyme, bay leaves, juniper berries, and peppercorns in a small bowl and mix well. Sprinkle the salt mixture over one side of the duck and rub it in with your fingertips. Turn and sprinkle the second side with the remaining salt mixture, rubbing it in. Cover and refrigerate overnight, or up to 2 days. Remove the duck from the baking dish and brush off the salt and seasonings.

Preheat the oven to 225°F (110°C).

Place the duck legs snugly in a single layer in a terrine or casserole. In a saucepan, melt the duck fat over medium heat. Pour the melted fat over the duck legs; they must be thoroughly covered in fat.

Bake until the duck legs are easily pierced with a knife, 2½–3 hours. Let the duck legs cool to room temperature in the fat. Pack the duck into a container and cover it with the fat. You may find a thin layer of concentrated gel at the bottom of the pan once the meat and fat have cooled. Save this in another container or a freezer bag. It is full of intense flavor that can be added to cassoulet or used to enrich sauces and soups. It is

continued on next page

SERVES 4

for the duck confit

4 duck legs with thighs

3 Tbsp sea salt

2 cloves garlic, crushed

3 fresh thyme sprigs

2 fresh or 1 dried bay leaf

1 tsp juniper berries, crushed

1 tsp black peppercorns, crushed

4 cups (29 oz/910 g) duck fat

for the sandwiches

About ½ cup (2½ oz/45 g) cornichons, thinly sliced

8 soft sandwich rolls, halved crosswise

a secret weapon for home cooks, the kind that restaurant kitchens have on hand all the time. The fat-sealed confit can be covered and stored in the refrigerator for up to 3 weeks.

When ready to use, remove the legs from the fat, scraping the fat from the legs and reserving it as it can be used again. Cut each duck leg at the joint where it meets the thigh. Working in batches, add 1 tablespoon of the reserved duck fat to a frying pan and add the legs and thighs, skin side down. Cook the duck over medium-high heat, turning it often, until the skin is crisp and golden, about 10 minutes. Remember, the duck was already cooked in the duck fat, so now you are only crisping it and warming it through.

To make the sandwiches, bone the legs, shred the meat, and chop the skin. Tuck equal amounts of the warm meat and skin and cornichons into the rolls. Serve at once.

RENDERING FAT

Rendering is the process of taking fatty meat scraps or pieces of solid fat, such as fatback, and heating them until the fat melts and separates from the meat or the fat simply melts. The resulting purified fat can then be stored and used in cooking in place of butter or oil. Beef tallow, poultry schmaltz, pork lard, and duck fat are the most common rendered fats.

In the home kitchen, you can also render fat from bones or carcasses. Combine them (roast them first, if you like) in a stockpot with aromatic vegetables and water to cover and simmer for 6–24 hours, then strain and chill the liquid. The rendered fat will solidify on the surface of the chilled liquid. Peel or spoon off the fat and use the liquid as stock. To make a purer fat, gently melt the chilled fat, rechill it, and then peel off only the top layer of the fat. The fat will keep in an airtight container in the refrigerator for up to 2 weeks or in the freezer for up to several months.

KIDNEYS in MUSTARD SAUCE

Offal, also called variety meats, remains an important part of French cooking at home and in brasseries. Kidneys, which I frequently bought and cooked as a young wife and mother, have become scarce in the United States. And so, whenever I see them on a menu in France, I order them. I recently had an especially fine version at a hotel restaurant in Fréjus, on the Mediterranean. After checking the posted menu, the opportunity to have rognons à la moutarde *was nearly as strong a draw as the shaded terrace overlooking the sea. I recommend veal kidneys, which are mildly flavored; any butcher can special order them. Serve this dish with plenty of bread for soaking up the sauce.*

Trim the kidneys, removing the hard white core of fat and discarding it. Cut the kidneys into slices or pieces about 1 inch (2.5 cm) thick. They will be irregular, but this is fine.

In a frying pan, melt 2 tablespoons of the butter over medium-high heat. When it foams, add the kidneys, sprinkle with the salt and pepper, and cook, turning them once or twice, until browned but still pink inside, 5–7 minutes. Cut one open to test. Be careful not to overcook. With a slotted spoon, transfer the kidneys to a bowl. Pour off all but 1 teaspoon of the pan juices.

Add the remaining 1 tablespoon butter and the shallot to the pan and sauté over medium heat until softened, 1–2 minutes. Add the mushrooms and sauté until they release their liquid, 3–4 minutes. Continue to cook until all but 1 tablespoon of the pan juices have evaporated. With a slotted spoon, add the mushroom mixture to the kidneys and set aside.

Stir the mustard into the remaining pan juices, then gradually pour in the wine, whisking until combined. Simmer over medium heat until slightly thickened, 1–2 minutes. Stir in ½ cup (4 fl oz/ 125 ml) of the crème fraîche, raise the heat to medium-high, and cook until the sauce is reduced to about ½ cup (4 fl oz/125 ml). Stir in the kidneys and mushrooms, without any collected juices, and simmer, stirring often, until warmed through, about 2 minutes. If the sauce seems too thick, stir in more crème fraîche. Taste and adjust the seasoning. Ladle into a serving bowl and serve at once.

SERVES 2

1–1¼ lb (500–625 g) veal kidneys

3 Tbsp unsalted butter

½ tsp sea salt

½ tsp freshly ground pepper

5 Tbsp (2 oz/60 g) minced shallot

8 large white or cremini mushrooms, brushed clean, stems trimmed, and thinly sliced

3 Tbsp Dijon mustard

⅔ cup (5 fl oz/160 ml) dry white wine such as Sauvignon Blanc

½–¾ cup (4–6 fl oz/125–180 ml) crème fraîche

CASSOULET

This is fundamentally a peasant dish from southwestern France, where it is made in dozens of versions, some loaded with different preserved and fresh meats and others with only one or two. My friend Kate Hill, who has lived in Gascony in the heart of cassoulet country for many years and has written a book on the dish, taught me that sometimes less is more when it comes to packing meats into the final dish. Dried beans are always used, and they must hold their shape during the long cooking. Tarbais beans, which are cultivated and processed near the commune of Tarbes, in the Hautes-Pyrénées, are favored. In the United States, Rancho Gordo, a company based in Northern California, sells Tarbais-type beans labeled "cassoulet beans." In the absence of both types, white kidney beans can be substituted. Preparing the beans is perhaps the most important step in making cassoulet, as a rich, flavorful broth develops as they cook that infuses the entire dish.

To prepare the beans, tie the thyme, parsley, and bay leaves together with kitchen string to make a bouquet garni.

Cut the pork belly crosswise into 1-inch (2.5-cm) slices. Roll up each slice and tie it with kitchen string.

In a Dutch oven with a lid, place the bouquet garni, pork belly, beans, leeks, celery, onion with the cloves, carrot, garlic, peppercorns, pancetta, and the pig's foot, if using. Add water to cover by 2 inches (5 cm) and bring to a boil over medium-high heat. Reduce the heat to low and simmer, partially covered, until the beans are barely tender and the broth is slightly opaque and flavorful, about 1 hour. At this point, you can add about 2 teaspoons salt and a little pepper. Remember, the beans will ultimately finish cooking in the oven as part of the cassoulet, so do not overcook them at this point.

While the beans are cooking, scrape off and reserve the fat in which the confit duck legs are packed. Cut each duck leg at the joint where it meets the thigh. Working in batches, add

continued on next page

SERVES 8

for the beans

6 fresh thyme sprigs

6 fresh parsley sprigs

2 fresh or 1 dried bay leaf

¼ lb (125 g) skin-on pork belly

2 lb (1 kg) dried Tarbais or cassoulet beans, soaked overnight in cold water and drained

2 leeks, white and pale green parts

2 ribs celery, cut in half crosswise

1 yellow onion, stuck with 5 whole cloves

1 large carrot, peeled

2 cloves garlic, crushed

➡

1 tablespoon of the reserved duck fat to a frying pan and add the legs and thighs, skin side down. Cook the duck over medium-high heat, turning it often, until the skin is crisp and golden, about 10 minutes. Transfer to a large plate and set aside.

Pour off all but 1 tablespoon of the fat from the frying pan, reserving it for another use. Add the sausages and cook over medium heat until cooked through and lightly browned, 12–15 minutes. Cut in half crosswise and set aside. Again, reserve the fat for another use.

Preheat the oven to 300°F (150°C). Remove and discard the bouquet garni. Remove the cloves from the onion, then finely chop the onion and return it to the beans. Remove and chop the carrot, the celery, and the white parts of the leeks (discard the more fibrous green parts) and return them to the beans.

Remove the rolled pork belly pieces and snip and discard the string. Mince the belly and return half of it to the beans. Set the remainder aside. Remove the pig's foot, if using, then remove and mince its meat and return it to the beans. Discard the bones and skin.

Taste the broth and adjust the seasoning. The broth should be quite flavorful but not overly salty.

Select a deep 6½–7-qt (6.2–6.6-l) casserole or baking dish. Using a slotted spoon, ladle in enough beans to create a layer 1 inch (2.5 cm) deep. Top with the confit pieces, followed by another 1-inch (2.5-cm) layer of beans. Cover with the sausages, followed by a final layer of beans. Sprinkle the top with the reserved pork belly, then ladle in enough broth to cover the beans by about ½ inch (12 mm). Reserve the remaining broth for basting.

Transfer to the oven and bake, uncovered. During the first hour of cooking, baste the top of the cassoulet as needed with its cooking broth. During the second hour, break through the crust with a wooden spoon to open it up and baste the cassoulet. Repeat two or three more times during the second and third hours and baste as needed with either the cooking broth or the reserved bean broth. Bake until the beans are meltingly tender, a crispy browned crust has formed, and the broth is bubbling along the sides, 2½–3 hours total.

Remove from the oven and serve directly from the casserole, making sure each serving includes a piece of duck confit and sausage.

1 tsp black peppercorns

¼ lb (125 g) pancetta, in a single piece

1 pig's foot (optional)

Sea salt

Freshly ground pepper

6 confit duck legs with their fat, homemade (page 153) or purchased

5 Toulouse or mild Italian sausages

LAMB with FLAGEOLET BEANS

The small, creamy white to light green beans known as flageolets are the classic accompaniment to lamb — with good reason. The beans, simmered with herbs and cooked until tender but not falling apart, mingle on the plate with the juice of the lamb, making a simple but aromatic pairing.

Pick over the beans, discarding any misshapen beans, stones, or other odd particles. Rinse under running cold water and drain. Put the beans in a large saucepan and add cold water to cover by 1½ inches (4 cm). Add the winter savory, bay leaves, and 1 teaspoon of the salt and bring to a boil over high heat. Reduce the heat to low, cover, and simmer until the beans are tender to the bite, 1½–2 hours. Let the beans stand in their cooking liquid until ready to serve.

Meanwhile, preheat the oven to 400°F (200°C).

Rub the lamb shanks all over with the remaining ½ teaspoon salt and the pepper. Place the shanks on a baking sheet and roast until browned and much of the fat is released, 20–30 minutes.

In a Dutch oven large enough to hold the shanks in a single layer, heat the oil over medium-high heat. Add the onion and sauté until translucent, about 2 minutes. Add the garlic and sauté for 1 minute longer. Add the tomatoes and their juice, thyme, and rosemary, stirring to combine. Add the lamb shanks, cover, and bake until the meat pulls back from the bones, 1½–2 hours. Discard the bay leaves.

Warm the beans over low heat until warmed through, about 10 minutes. Taste and adjust the seasoning. Using a slotted spoon, spoon the beans and the tomato mixture onto a platter and top with the lamb shanks. Serve at once.

SERVES 4

1 cup (7 oz/220 g) dried flageolet beans

2 Tbsp minced fresh winter savory or 1 tsp dried

2 fresh or 1 dried bay leaf

1½ tsp sea salt

4 lamb shanks, ¾–1 lb (375–500 g) each

1 tsp freshly ground pepper

2 Tbsp extra-virgin olive oil

½ yellow onion, minced

2 cloves garlic, minced

1 can (14½ oz/411 g) canned plum tomatoes, chopped, with their juice

1 tsp fresh thyme leaves

½ tsp minced fresh rosemary

STUFFED LAMB, MICHOUI-STYLE

*Michoui is a North African feast that features a whole lamb stuffed with rice
and vegetables and roasted on a spit. It has become popular in southern France, a
large lamb-producing region, where it is often the centerpiece of local community fêtes.
Although this is a simplified version, it has the flavors of that grand feast. You will
likely need to special order the lamb breast. Be sure to ask the butcher to cut a pocket
(a slit between the rib bones and the meaty flap) for holding the stuffing.*

Preheat the oven to 350°F (180°C).

In a frying pan, heat 2 tablespoons of the oil over high heat. Add
the onion and sauté until translucent, about 2 minutes. Add the
zucchini, eggplant, bell pepper, and garlic and sauté until the
eggplant is just tender, about 4 minutes, adding more oil if needed.
Transfer to a bowl, add the rice, parsley, thyme, rosemary, 1 teaspoon salt, ½ teaspoon black pepper, and ¼ teaspoon cayenne, and
mix well. Taste and adjust the seasoning.

In a small bowl, stir together 1 teaspoon each salt and black
pepper, ¼ teaspoon cayenne, and the cumin. Rub the lamb
breast inside and out with the mixture. Fill the pocket with the
stuffing, being careful not to overstuff. Using a poultry needle
and kitchen string, sew the pocket closed. Place the stuffed
breast on a rack in a roasting pan. Put any leftover stuffing in
a covered baking dish and bake for 30 minutes before serving.

Roast the lamb, basting occasionally with the remaining
2 tablespoons oil, until the meat pulls back from the bones,
the surface is golden, and the meat is easily pierced with a
fork, about 1½ hours. Remove from the oven, cover loosely
with aluminum foil, and let stand for 10 minutes.

To carve, cut between the first and second ribs for the first
serving. Remove to a platter or plate with a spatula. Continue
slicing and serving as you go. Serve at once with the *harissa*.

SERVES 6–8

4 Tbsp (2 fl oz/60 ml)
extra-virgin olive oil,
plus oil as needed

½ yellow onion, minced

2 zucchini, finely chopped

½ eggplant, cut into
½-inch (12-mm) cubes

½ red bell pepper, seeded
and finely chopped

4 cloves garlic, minced

1 cup (5 oz/155 g) cooked
long-grain rice, cold

¼ cup (⅓ oz/10 g) chopped
fresh flat-leaf parsley

2 tsp fresh thyme leaves

½ tsp minced
fresh rosemary

Sea salt, freshly
ground black pepper,
and cayenne pepper

1 tsp ground cumin

1 bone-in lamb breast,
about 3 lb (1.5 kg),
with cut pocket

Harissa for serving

THE TRANSHUMANCE

The French have a fierce dedication to their
traditions of sustainability. One instance is the
continuation and resurgence of the transhumance,
that centuries-old practice of taking the sheep in
June from the valleys of southern France to the
high mountain pastures to spend the summers,
then bringing them back again in September to
shelter and lamb in the protection of the valleys.
Archaeological evidence shows that shepherds
and their sheep have plied the *drailes*, or "trails,"
that crisscross France from the southern lowland
to the French Alps since Roman times.

The grand *troupeaux*, or "herds," each with
sheep numbering in the thousands, are guided by
men and dogs along the pathways of their ancestors,
passing through towns and villages, across mead-
ows and ravines to reach their destinations, a trek
that can take up to two weeks. The guides sleep out
under the stars with the animals, meals are cooked
over open fires, and the provisions and cookware are
brought along in trucks.

At one point, in the 1980s, the number of
troupeaux making the trek was declining in favor
of transporting the animals by trucks. But it was
found the animals didn't thrive on the long truck
journey, and the villagers along the way regretted
the loss of the familiar passage. Today, fêtes are
held in many villages and towns when the sheep
pass through, and there are even organizations
that arrange amateur participation, so the layperson
can travel with the *troupeaux* for a day or two.

GUINEA HEN with SAUTÉED QUINCE, APPLES & PEARS

Fall is my favorite time to cook guinea hen because of the trio of fruits that come into season then—pears, apples, and quinces. If you've never eaten guinea hen, seek it out and cook it. It is more flavorful than chicken or pheasant, and although it is lean, it isn't dry. While readily available at open markets and butcher shops in France, I can only get it in California by special order. Any leftovers can be warmed to top a frisée salad, plus the carcass makes a superb broth (page 166). To accompany the guinea hen and fruit, I serve polenta or couscous.

Preheat the oven to 350°F (180°C).

If your guinea hen comes with the head and feet intact, chop these off with a heavy knife or cleaver and reserve them to make broth (page 166). Rinse and pat the guinea hen dry. Rub the guinea hen, inside and out, with the whole sage sprigs, then rub the hen, inside and out, with the salt and pepper, including rubbing some under the skin. Place the sage sprigs in the cavity, along with the heart and liver, if available. With kitchen string, tie the legs together.

In a Dutch oven, melt the butter over medium-high heat. When it foams, add the guinea hen, breast side up, and cook until browned on the bottom, 4–5 minutes. Flip and cook until the second side is browned, 4–5 minutes longer. Turn the bird breast side up, add ½ cup (4 fl oz/125 ml) water, and cover the pot.

Bake the guinea hen, basting once or twice with the pan juices, until the juice runs clear when the deepest point behind the thigh is pierced with a knife tip, or until an instant-read thermometer inserted into the same spot reads 160°F (71°C), about 1 hour. Transfer the guinea hen to a carving board, cover loosely with aluminum foil, and let rest for 10 minutes before carving.

continued on next page

SERVES 3-4

1 guinea hen, 2½–3 lb (1.25–1.5 kg), preferably with the heart and liver

6 fresh sage sprigs

1 tsp coarse sea salt, crushed

1 tsp freshly ground pepper

2 Tbsp unsalted butter

Meanwhile, about 10 minutes before the guinea hen comes out of the oven, prepare the fruit: In a large frying pan, melt the butter over medium-high heat. When it foams, add the quinces and onion and sauté, turning the fruit slices once or twice, until golden and just barely soft when pricked with the tip of a knife, about 8 minutes. Add the apples, pears, and salt. Cook, turning, until just tender, about 4 minutes. Cover to keep warm.

Remove the foil from the guinea hen. Carve the breast from the bone and cut into slices, then cut off the wings and the legs with thighs attached.

Arrange the sliced breast on a warmed platter, add the fruits (warming them beforehand if they have cooled too much), and add the wings and legs with thighs attached. Pour any collected juices from the carving board back into the Dutch oven, heat over medium-high heat, pour over the meat and fruits, and serve.

for the fruit

2 Tbsp unsalted butter

2 quinces, peeled, cored, and cut into ½-inch (12-mm) slices

½ yellow onion, thinly sliced

2 apples such as Golden Delicious, Gala, or Granny Smith, unpeeled, cored and cut into ½-inch (12-mm) slices

2 firm, ripe pears such as Bosc or Red Bartlett, unpeeled, cored and cut into ½-inch (12-mm) slices

½ tsp fine sea salt

EASY BROTH BASICS

Homemade broth is a useful item to have in your freezer, ready to use when you need it, and it is easy to make. A single chicken carcass left over from roasting chicken is enough to make a quart (liter) of broth, for example. Or you can freeze leftover carcasses or bones to make larger batches.

Take some bones—chicken, guinea hen, duck, pork, lamb, veal—roasted or not, put them in a large pot, and cover with a goodly amount of water. Add some aromatics—carrots, celery, onion, leeks, peppercorns, a bouquet garni of parsley and thyme sprigs and a bay leaf—bring to a boil over medium-high heat, and skim off and discard the froth that comes to the surface. Reduce the heat to low and simmer until the bones, vegetables, and aromatics have rendered their flavor and the water has reduced to a broth, 3–4 hours. Strain through a chinois or fine-mesh sieve and discard the solids. Taste the broth and add sea salt, if you like.

You can also use the carcass of cooked poultry, which adds character to the broth because it has some additional flavoring from its previous cooking. You can create broth from the bones of cooked pork or lamb, as well. Beef broth is best purposefully prepared by roasting about 10 lb (5 kg) assorted meaty bones like ribs and shanks, as well as marrowbones, before putting them into the stockpot. Beef broth also needs to simmer longer, up to 12 hours or more. Fish stock, also known as *fumet,* (page 260) takes less time to cook and includes wine.

Homemade broth will lend backbone to whatever dish you are using it in. I make it when I have a leftover carcass or bones, then I freeze it in the portion sizes I am most likely to use. Besides being an important ingredient in many dishes, it is also good to drink on its own, seasoned with a little salt and pepper.

THE ESSENTIAL PIG

At one time, every French farm family kept at least one pig to raise over the year to provide a wealth of provisions for the family. Typically, a piglet would be purchased from an *éleveur de cochons*, someone who kept breeding sows. When we lived in Provence and raised goats and made cheese, we also kept a sow—who, as noted earlier, we named Lucretia—and we sold the baby pigs, called feeder pigs, to local families. We fed Lucretia a diet of protein-rich whey (left over from cheese making) mixed with bran, various windfalls like fruits and almonds, and feed pellets, and we took her on walks so she could root and forage.

The French like their pigs for provisions to be big, 300 pounds (135 kg) or more, and every little bit is used. Legs become *jambon cru* (salt-cured hams), shoulders are made into roasts, bellies are seasoned and cured in salt, and the blood is captured to make *boudin noir* (blood sausage). Much of the meat, from scraps to meaty chunks, is combined with the fatback for sausages and pâtés. Leaf fat is saved for pastry making. Ears are pickled, feet and the head become headcheese, loins are turned into roasts or chops, and in the old days, the intestines were scrupulously cleaned and used as the casing for the sausages. Traditionally, as much of the meat as possible was preserved to provision the pantry throughout the year. Much of the renowned food of the French countryside is founded on some part of the pig.

HOMEMADE MERGUEZ

I once had a fantasy about being a butcher and specializing in charcuterie, and I am delighted to see so many women succeeding in this today. Rather than going to butchery school, I contented myself with replicating the tricks I learned while living in France, supplementing them with a class here and there. I especially like sausage making, and I've frequently joined with other sausage-making fanciers for a long morning of big-batch sausage making, frying up samples as we go for nourishment, downed with a little red wine and bread, of course. Not everyone has, or wants, a sausage stuffer to make filled links, so this recipe for merguez, a popular North African lamb sausage also favored in France, is for bulk sausage. I use it for making burgers, sliders, and meatballs, and to season egg dishes.

In a spice grinder or clean coffee grinder, combine the fennel, coriander, cumin, salt, and peppercorns and finely grind. Transfer the spices to a bowl and stir in the cinnamon, cayenne, and paprika. Store in an airtight container for up to 3 months.

To make the sausage, if using lamb shoulder, cut into 1-inch (2.5-cm) chunks and grind with a meat grinder filled with the medium plate. In a large bowl, combine the lamb, garlic, *harissa*, salt, and cayenne and mix thoroughly with your hands. Add 3 tablespoons of the spice mixture and mix well again with your hands. Cover with plastic wrap and refrigerate until the flavors blend, at least 2 hours, or up to overnight.

To check the seasoning of the sausage mixture, shape a tablespoon or so into a patty and fry it in a small frying pan over medium heat until cooked. Taste and adjust the seasoning of the uncooked sausage mixture if needed. It should be spicy but not overwhelmingly so. If not spicy enough for your taste, add a little more of the *harissa* or spice mixture.

Shape the sausage into patties or divide it into portion sizes of your choice for cooking, then store, tightly sealed, in the refrigerator for up to 4 days or in the freezer for up to 6 months.

MAKES 2 LB (1 KG)
BULK MERGUEZ

for the spices
2 Tbsp fennel seeds
2 Tbsp coriander seeds
1 Tbsp cumin seeds
1 Tbsp coarse sea salt
½ tsp black peppercorns
½ tsp ground cinnamon
½ tsp cayenne pepper
¼ cup (1 oz/30 g) sweet paprika

for the sausage
2 lb (1 kg) ground lamb or boneless lamb shoulder

5 cloves garlic, minced
2 Tbsp harissa
1 Tbsp coarse sea salt
½ tsp cayenne pepper

GRILLED PORK BELLY

The French are noted for using all parts of the pig in delicious and creative ways. I'd always thought of the pork belly as the source of French-style pancetta, well seasoned with herbs and peppers, rolled, and cured, or as slowly braised. I had never considered grilling pork belly until I saw it sliced, packaged, and labeled bon pour le grillade *in the meat department of a French supermarket. My husband and I decided we'd try it and discovered how easy and good it was. Since then, I've experimented with different versions, sometimes cut into strips and other times in a whole piece, as it is here. When cut into bite-size pieces, the grilled pork belly makes a tasty hors d'oeuvre. Ask the butcher to remove the skin for you, or do it yourself with a sharp knife.*

Rub the pork belly all over with the salt, pepper, and herbes de Provence.

In a small bowl, stir together the oil and vinegar. Place the pork belly in a baking dish and pour the oil and vinegar over the top, turning the pork belly several times to coat. Let stand at room temperature for 2 hours, turning once or twice.

Prepare a charcoal or wood fire in a grill or preheat a gas grill. When the grill is hot, toss on a handful of grapevine prunings, if you have them (page 172).

Remove the pork belly from the marinade, reserving the marinade for basting. Grill the pork belly, turning often and basting with the reserved marinade for the first 5 minutes of cooking. Continue to grill until the pork is firm to the touch and is crispy golden, about 10 minutes total. Transfer to a carving board and let rest for 5 minutes, loosely covered with aluminum foil.

Cut crosswise into ¼-inch (6-mm) slices or cut into bite-size cubes. Transfer to a platter and serve at once.

SERVES 6-8

2 lb (1 kg) skinless pork belly, in a single piece

½ tsp sea salt

¼ tsp freshly ground pepper

¼ tsp herbes de Provence

¼ cup (2 fl oz/60 ml) extra-virgin olive oil

2 Tbsp red wine vinegar

GRILLING WITH GRAPEVINE PRUNINGS

In France, wherever grapes are grown, the favored fuel for grilling is grapevine trunks, or failing those, grapevine prunings, called *sarments*. Even Michelin-starred restaurants tout "grilled over *sarments*" on their menus. Of course, the trunks are only available when a vineyard has been pulled out. In that case, the pulled vines are stacked and carefully guarded until needed. My neighbor in France pulled out an old vineyard in order to plant olive trees, and for several years, I had a healthy supply of grapevines.

Grapevine trunks can be hard to come by. However, every year, without fail, there are prunings. The stalks and prunings burn very hot, but briefly, and add a smoky, woodsy flavor to steaks, chops, and sausages, and to the occasional pork belly, sliced or whole (page 171).

I don't have wine grapes at my home in California, but I do have a large arbor of table grapes. Every winter I save the prunings and cut them into 6-inch (15-cm) lengths to use for grilling throughout the year.

I have a limited supply of grapevine prunings. To make the most of them, I build a wood or charcoal fire and lay a big handful of *sarments* on top of the coals just before putting the meat on.

ROAST CHICKEN & POTATOES
with DRIPPINGS

Rotisserie chickens turn on spits in open markets and in front of butcher shops throughout France, often with their juices dripping onto the potatoes cooking below. When you choose your chicken, you are asked if you'd like potatoes as well. If you answer yes, which I always do, potatoes and juices (and sometimes onions and peppers) are ladled into a heatproof bag along with the chicken. At home, to replicate those jus-bathed potatoes, I position the chicken on a rack in a roasting pan, with the potatoes beneath.

Preheat the oven to 350°F (180°C). Rub the chicken, inside and out, with the salt, pepper, and the rosemary and thyme sprigs, then place the sprigs and the bay leaves in the cavity. Using kitchen string, tie the drumsticks together.

Place the chicken on a rack in a roasting pan just large enough to hold it and roast, uncovered, for 30 minutes.

Meanwhile, put the potatoes in a large saucepan, add water to cover by 1 inch (2.5 cm), and bring to a boil over medium-high heat. Reduce the heat to medium, cover, and cook until the potatoes are just beginning to become tender, about 15 minutes. Drain and set aside.

Remove the roasting pan from the oven, lift out the chicken and rack, and place the potatoes, onion, and peppers in the pan. Dot the vegetables with ½ tablespoon of the butter, replace the chicken and rack, and rub the chicken all over with the remaining ½ tablespoon butter. Continue to roast until the chicken is golden brown and the juice runs clear when a thigh is pierced with a knife tip, or an instant-read thermometer inserted into a thigh registers 165°F (74°C), and the potatoes are tender when pierced with the knife, about 45 minutes. Transfer the chicken to a carving board and let rest for 10 minutes.

To serve, carve the chicken and pour any collected carving juices back into the pan. Arrange the chicken on a platter, surround it with the vegetables, and drizzle the pan juices over the chicken.

SERVES 6

1 whole chicken, about 3½ lb (1.75 kg)

2 tsp sea salt

2 tsp freshly ground pepper

3–4 fresh rosemary sprigs

3–4 fresh thyme sprigs

2 fresh or 1 dried bay leaf

8–10 small Yukon gold potatoes, peeled or unpeeled

1 large yellow onion, coarsely chopped

2 red sweet peppers such as bell, seeded and cut lengthwise into ½-inch (12-mm) strips

1 Tbsp unsalted butter, at room temperature

BEEF BRAISED in RED WINE & BONE MARROW

Beef marrow is one of those primal foods that is frequently overlooked, but which the French have always prized. Ask the butcher to saw the bones lengthwise in half, so the marrow steams gently as the bones sit atop the slowly cooking beef.

Preheat the oven to 325°F (165°C). In a large Dutch oven, heat the oil over medium-high heat. Add the lardons, reduce the heat to medium, and sauté until the lardons are just golden and have rendered their fat, about 5 minutes. Add the onion and sauté until translucent, about 3 minutes. With a slotted spoon, transfer the lardons and onion to a bowl.

Pat the beef dry and season with 1 teaspoon salt and ½ teaspoon pepper. Return the pot to medium-high heat and, working in batches to avoid crowding, add the meat and cook, turning several times, until browned on all sides, about 10 minutes. Transfer to a bowl and repeat until all of the meat is browned.

Return the meat to the pot, sprinkle with the flour, and cook over medium-high heat, turning constantly, until the flour is browned. Slowly drizzle in the wine and deglaze the pan by scraping up any bits that cling to the bottom. Return the lardons, onion, and any collected juices to the pot. Add the carrots, tomatoes, broth, celery, thyme, and bay leaves. Bring to a boil, cover, and place in the oven.

Meanwhile, prepare the bone marrow: Fill a large bowl with ice water and soak the marrowbones for 30 minutes to draw out any residual blood. Remove the bones, pat dry, and set aside.

When the beef has cooked 1½ hours, lay the marrowbones, cut side up, on top and ladle a little braising liquid over them. Re-cover and continue to cook until the beef is fork-tender, 1½–2 hours longer.

Remove the marrowbones and keep warm. Skim off and discard the fat from the braising liquid, then divide the braise evenly among 4 plates. Garnish each serving with a split marrowbone and 2–3 baguette slices and serve.

SERVES 4

1 Tbsp extra-virgin olive oil

2 oz (60 g) lardons, or 3 slices thick-cut bacon, cut crosswise into thin slices

½ yellow onion, chopped

1½ lb (750 g) boneless beef chuck, cut into 2-inch (5-cm) cubes

Sea salt and freshly ground pepper

1 Tbsp all-purpose flour

1 cup (8 fl oz/250 ml) dry red wine

6 carrots, peeled and cut into 1-inch (2.5-cm) lengths

2 cups (12 oz/375 g) chopped plum tomatoes, with their juice

2 cups (16 fl oz/500 ml) beef broth, homemade (page 166) or purchased

2 ribs celery, chopped

3 fresh thyme sprigs

2 fresh or 1 dried bay leaf

4 beef marrowbones, each about 4 inches (10 cm) long, halved lengthwise

8–12 slices baguette, grilled or toasted

BLANQUETTE de VEAU

One of the old-fashioned dishes of French cooking — and one of my favorites — this veal stew in cream sauce remains so embedded in French culture that nearly every supermarket or butcher shop sells veau pour blanquette, a preassembled selection of cuts and bones. You tell the butcher how many people you are serving, and he or she gives you the perfect combination. Serve the stew with steamed rice and, if desired, garnish it with glacéed pearl onions (page 103) and sautéed quartered mushrooms.

Tie the thyme, parsley, and bay leaves together with kitchen string to make a bouquet garni. Place the shank, breast, and stew meat in a large stockpot. Add the carrots, onion, salt, peppercorns, bouquet garni, and cold water to cover by at least 2 inches (5 cm). Bring to a boil over medium-high heat, skimming off any foam that forms on the surface until it stops forming, about 30 minutes. Cover partially, reduce the heat to medium-low, and simmer until the meat is tender and pulls back from the bone, 1–1½ hours total.

With a slotted spoon, transfer the meat and carrots to a plate. Discard the bouquet garni. Strain the cooking liquid through a chinois or fine-mesh sieve placed over a large pitcher. You should have about 4 cups (32 fl oz/1 l). If necessary, add a little water.

In a saucepan, melt the butter over medium heat. Remove from the heat and whisk in the flour to make a paste. Return to the heat and whisk in the cooking liquid. Continue cooking, stirring often, until slightly thickened, about 10 minutes. Remove from the heat.

Meanwhile, in a bowl, whisk together the crème fraîche and egg yolk. Whisk in ½ cup (4 fl oz/125 ml) of the thickened cooking liquid and the lemon juice. Return the cooking liquid to medium heat and slowly whisk in the egg mixture to make a thick sauce. Taste and adjust the seasoning. Add the meat and carrots, reserving any accumulated juices for another use. Simmer, turning often, until the meat is warmed through, about 10 minutes.

Ladle the stew into a serving bowl or onto a platter. Garnish with a sprig or two of parsley. Serve at once.

SERVES 6-8

1 fresh thyme sprig

3 fresh flat-leaf parsley sprigs, plus 1–2 sprigs for garnish

2 fresh or 1 dried bay leaf

1 veal shank, about 1 lb (500 g)

1 lb (500 g) boneless veal breast, cut into 2-inch (5-cm) pieces

1 lb (500 g) veal stew meat, or 1 lb (500 g) veal shoulder, cut into 2-inch (5-cm) pieces

2 carrots, peeled and cut into ½-inch (12-mm) rounds

1 yellow onion, coarsely chopped

3 tsp sea salt

5 black peppercorns

2 Tbsp unsalted butter

2 Tbsp all-purpose flour

About 1 cup (8 fl oz/250 ml) crème fraîche

1 large egg yolk

2 Tbsp fresh lemon juice

FROZEN MERINGUES & FRESH APRICOTS

Françoise, a lovely, creative, and kind neighbor in France, recently passed away, but she left me with many rich memories of shared dishes and recipes. This fancy yet simple-to-make dessert is one of them. In France, just about every pâtisserie and boulangerie sells ready-made meringues, the hard, crunchy kind. You can find them in this country, as well, and though they are usually a smaller cookie size, they work well in this recipe. In case you cannot find them, I have included a recipe here.

In a large bowl, using an electric beater, beat the cream until stiff peaks form, about 6 minutes. Slowly beat in the sugar until combined.

Break the meringues into bite-size or slightly larger pieces. It doesn't matter if they are all different sizes. Fold these into the whipped cream along with the chopped apricots. You will have a thick, lumpy mass.

Spoon into a freezer-safe container with a lid and freeze overnight, or up to 1 week.

Using a large spoon, spoon into dessert bowls or glasses and garnish with the apricot slices.

SERVES 4

2 cups (16 fl oz/500 ml) heavy cream

2 Tbsp sugar

8–10 cookie-type hard meringues, each about 2 inches (5 cm) wide, or 1 recipe Hard Meringues (recipe follows)

6 apricots, pitted and coarsely chopped, plus 2 apricots, pitted and sliced, for garnish

HARD MERINGUES

Preheat the oven to 180°F (82°C). Line a baking sheet with parchment paper. In a large bowl, using an electric beater, beat together the sugar and egg whites until shiny peaks form that hold their shape, about 15 minutes. Using the tip of a knife, scrape the vanilla seeds into the bowl, then add the salt and beat just until combined.

Spoon tablespoonfuls of the meringue onto the prepared baking sheet, spacing them 1 inch (2.5 cm) apart. Bake the meringues until they feel light, the bottoms are hard, and the tops sound hollow when tapped, about 4 hours. Turn off the oven and let the meringues rest in the oven overnight. Use immediately, or transfer to a paper bag and store in a dry location for up to 3 days.

1¼ cups (10 oz/315 g) sugar

5 large egg whites

1-inch (2.5-cm) piece vanilla bean, split lengthwise

⅛ teaspoon sea salt

CREPES

Crepes, those deliciously thin French pancakes, are exceedingly versatile. You can serve them warm with an assortment of jams, butter, and fresh fruit, or sprinkled with sugar, folded into quarters, and drizzled with melted butter for breakfast. On the sweet side, they can be filled with honey, Nutella, or nuts and rolled or folded into quarters, garnished with whipped cream, ice cream, chocolate syrup, or fresh fruits—the list is endless. The same is true for savory crepes. Fillings include cheese, lardons, ham, Spinach à la Crème (page 63), fried eggs, mushrooms, or shellfish, and a drizzle of béchamel sauce or melted butter for garnish. I like to cover savory crepes with béchamel sauce, top them with shredded Gruyère, and bake them until the top is golden brown and bubbling.

Put the milk in a large bowl. Gradually add the flour, whisking thoroughly to prevent any lumps from forming. Add the salt, followed by the eggs, whisking well until a thin batter forms.

Refrigerate the batter for 30 minutes to settle, then remove from the refrigerator and whisk again.

In an 8-inch (20-cm) nonstick frying pan or crepe pan, melt 1 teaspoon of the butter over medium-high heat. When it foams, add 2 tablespoons of the batter (I fill up a ¼-cup/2–fl oz/60 ml measure halfway) and quickly tilt the pan to cover the bottom with a thin layer of the batter. Cook until the edges of the crepe begin to curl and bubbles begin to form, about 1 minute. Using a spatula, turn and cook the other side until pale golden, a few seconds longer. Transfer to a plate and repeat with the remaining batter, adding just enough butter to the pan each time to prevent sticking. As the crepes are done, stack them and cover them with a dish towel to keep them warm if serving right away. To store the crepes, let them cool, then stack them between layers of wax paper, wrap in plastic wrap, and refrigerate for up to 3 days; or wrap the stacked crepes in aluminum foil, place in a lock-top plastic bag, and freeze for up to 2 months.

MAKES ABOUT
18 CREPES

1 cup (8 fl oz/250 ml) whole milk

¾ cup (4 oz/125 g) all-purpose flour

¼ tsp sea salt

2 large eggs

2 Tbsp unsalted butter

CRÈME BRÛLÉE with LAVENDER

The joy of keeping chickens is an abundance of fresh eggs, which perhaps accounts for the numerous French dishes, from soufflés to quiches to custards, that rely on them. The better your eggs, the better your finished dish will be.

Preheat the oven to 325°F (165°C). Have ready four ¾-cup (6–fl oz/180-ml) ramekins and a broiler-proof baking dish just large enough to hold the ramekins.

In a saucepan, combine the cream and granulated sugar and cook over medium-high heat, stirring, until the sugar melts and small bubbles appear around the edges, 3–4 minutes. Remove from the heat, add the vanilla bean and dried lavender blossoms, and let stand for 35–40 minutes.

Remove and discard the vanilla bean and strain the mixture through a chinois or fine-mesh sieve. In a large bowl, whisk together the egg yolks until thickened, about 2 minutes. Gradually whisk the cream mixture into the egg yolks and strain again. Pour the custard into the ramekins, filling to within ¼ inch (6 mm) of the rim.

Bring a kettle of water to a boil. Place the ramekins in the baking dish. Pour boiling water into the dish to come halfway up the sides of the ramekins. Bake the custards until set but still jiggly in the center and a pale gold skin has formed on the top, 35–40 minutes.

Transfer the baking dish to a wire rack and let the custards cool slightly. Remove the ramekins and let cool to room temperature. Refrigerate until well chilled, at least 4 hours, or up to overnight.

When ready to serve, preheat the broiler. Put the brown sugar into a fine-mesh sieve and, using a spoon, push it through the sieve, evenly sprinkling the tops of the custards. Return the ramekins to the baking dish, pour cold water around them, and add several ice cubes. Broil until the sugar melts and caramelizes, 2–3 minutes. Alternatively, caramelize the sugar with a kitchen torch.

Transfer the custards to a wire rack. Let cool until the sugar hardens, about 10 minutes. Garnish with the lavender sprigs and serve.

SERVES 4

2 cups (16 fl oz/500 ml) heavy cream

¼ cup (2 oz/60 g) granulated sugar

1-inch (2.5-cm) piece vanilla bean, split lengthwise

2 Tbsp dried culinary lavender blossoms (untreated)

4 large egg yolks

3 Tbsp firmly packed brown sugar

Ice cubes

4 culinary lavender sprigs (untreated), fresh or dried, for garnish

LARD PASTRY

I grew up using purchased lard to make pie pastries, just the way my grandmother taught me. In Provence, my neighbor Marie rendered leaf fat to make lard for her pastries. Then, lard fell out of fashion and I used margarine or butter, or a combination. However, lard is popular once again, which pleases me because it makes a truly flaky crust. The fat around the kidneys of pigs is called leaf fat. It is the finest and most tender, and the best for making pastry. Rendered fatback can be used as well, but it has a more pronounced flavor and is better for savory dishes. You can buy rendered leaf fat or you can purchase raw leaf fat and render your own (page 154). Some farmers' markets carry both, or you can buy them and lard from your butcher or online. This recipe is easily doubled for a double-crust pie or tart, such as the Swiss chard pie on page 58, and can be used for quiche on page 146.

In a bowl, whisk together the flour and salt. Cut the lard into chunks and, using a pastry cutter, work the lard into the flour until pea-size pieces form, about 5 minutes. Add 3 tablespoons of the ice water and mix with a fork. Add another tablespoon of the water, mix again, and pack the dough into a ball. If the dough is too crumbly to form a ball, break it apart and add more ice water. Wrap in plastic wrap and refrigerate for 30 minutes before rolling out.

The pastry will keep in the refrigerator for up 3 days; let sit at room temperature for several minutes to soften slightly before rolling out.

MAKES ONE 9-INCH
(23-CM) PIE CRUST

1½ cups (7½ oz/235 g) all-purpose flour

⅛ tsp fine sea salt

½ cup (3½ oz/105 g) tightly packed lard, preferably made from leaf fat, chilled

4–5 Tbsp ice water

HOMEMADE SALTED BUTTER

Butter used to be homemade when people kept cows, but we have, of course, become used to purchasing it. Once you've made your own, you may find it hard to go back. Pour organic heavy cream into a food processor and process until it begins to thicken, about 5 minutes. You will notice that some liquid is being squeezed out as the butter forms—that's buttermilk. When the cream is thick, pour off the buttermilk (reserve it for crème fraîche, below).

Using your hands, squeeze out the remaining liquid from the butter. Put the butter in a bowl and add coarse sel de Guérande *(page 271) to taste. I use about ½ teaspoon per 2 cups (1 lb/500 g) fresh butter. I love the way the salt crystals pop when the butter is spread on toast.*

HOMEMADE CRÈME FRAÎCHE

Crème fraîche is a secret weapon of French cooking. It is slightly soured cream and has a higher butterfat content than conventional sour cream, which means it won't curdle when used in cooking. It is perfect for adding to a pan sauce, finishing off a stew, or garnishing a soup or dessert. Commercially it is made by adding a mixture of bacteria cultures to heavy cream, but you can make it at home by adding 2 tablespoons buttermilk for each 1 cup (8 fl oz/250 ml) heavy cream. I suggest using organic products to keep it as close as possible to the original source. Stir the mixture well, cover, and let stand at room temperature overnight. Voilà, the next morning you will have crème fraîche. Keep it covered and store in the refrigerator for up to 5 days. When you want to replenish your supply, you can use your homemade crème fraîche as a starter instead of buttermilk.

GOAT'S MILK AUTREFOIS

In the old days, goat's milk was seen as extremely nutritious—good for both the old and the young—and it demanded a higher price than cow's milk. Cow's milk was brought into the villages directly after milking, in milk cans strapped onto donkeys or in carts pulled by donkeys or horses. The vendors would stop at a designated corner and ladle out the milk to customers. The goat's milk vendors simply brought the milking goat into the village and let people milk into their own containers, thus avoiding the whole (and very important) chore of cleaning and sanitizing the milk cans in an era of limited running water. So practical.

CHAPTER FOUR

THE FOREST
& FIELD

THE FOREST & FIELD

WILD THINGS

French tables are rife with wild ingredients gathered from the forest and fields, and the knowledge of clandestine locations of wild mushrooms, truffles, wild asparagus, leeks, strawberries, and currants is handed down through families. In France, foraging can be a profession, not just a pastime, and the great markets are well stocked with seasonal wild ingredients, including game. Wild game is especially popular during the months leading up to Christmas and New Year's, where still-feathered pheasant are festooned with red ribbons and hung outside butcher shops and even in supermarkets.

Hunting is a popular sport, and wild boar, upland birds, deer, and even small birds also make their way to the French table. In some regions, if you pop into a French bar around noon during the hunting season, chances are you'll see a slew of men in camouflage standing around and talking about their morning's quarry.

Many of my neighbors in Provence are hunters, so I have often been the happy recipient of whole pheasants or haunches and rib roasts of wild boar. I've never been offered the coveted game birds, *grive* and *bécasse*, although I've been invited to meals where they were served. The spoils of the day's hunt are braised, roasted, or grilled, or are turned into pâtés, terrines, and sausages that are then served throughout the year and, sometimes, given to friends. The charcuterie is usually seasoned with other wild ingredients, such as juniper, thyme, winter savory, and rosemary—the tastes of the forest.

Snails, the most humble of the hunted, are also a treasured ingredient, and they can be found on menus all over France, though today they are more likely to be farm raised.

Unlike foraging for truffles, foraging for mushrooms is rather democratic, and in many families, it is a tradition. Mushrooms have two seasons: fall, when you can find cèpes, chanterelles, hedgehogs, puffballs, and in Provence, *sanguins*; and spring, known primarily for morels and shaggy manes. All of these mushrooms have unique characteristics, and these are the only ones I forage. Other foragers, who are more knowledgeable and more daring than I, gather

additional, less readily identifiable types. Mushroom hunting can also be an important economic sideline for locals, who often sell a hundred or more kilos in a season. It's not surprising that communes have signs posted on the perimeters of their forests that say that mushroom hunting is for locals only.

Truffle hunting is highly specialized, and due to the enormous prices truffles bring (page 200), highly competitive. Dogs and pigs are used to sniff out the underground fungi. Some forest tracts are leased by individuals specifically for the right to hunt truffles, and other tracts of land, generally smaller, are planted with trees, primarily oaks, that have been inoculated with truffle spores. Some old-timers also plant acorns from wild trees that are known truffle producers. Truffle season begins in November and is generally over by mid-February, and although truffles can be purchased canned year-round, it is the fresh truffle that is by far the more desirable.

PURSLANE SALAD with ROASTED MARROWBONES & GROS SEL

Purslane, known as pourpier *in France, is a wild green succulent that grows in vineyards and gardens. During spring and summer, it can sometimes be found in the open markets in France and at farmers' markets in the United States. At my house in California, it comes up every year in the garden, along the edge of the lawn, and in the grape arbor. Farmers consider it a weed, but we cooks love the slightly tart, lemon flavor of its leaves, which makes an ideal counterpart to rich bone marrow. If you can't find purslane, use wild or baby arugula mixed with watercress.*

Fill a large bowl with ice water and soak the marrowbones for 30 minutes to draw out any residual blood.

Preheat the oven to 450°F (230°C). Remove the bones and pat dry. Place the bones, marrow side up, on a rimmed baking sheet. Roast until the marrow is hot and soft but not melting, about 10 minutes.

Separate the leaves and tender sprigs from the purslane stems, discarding the stems. You should have about 4 cups (4 oz/125 g). In a salad bowl, whisk together the shallots, oil, capers, lemon juice, ¼ teaspoon of the salt, and the ¼ teaspoon pepper. Add the purslane and toss to coat well.

Divide the salad and marrowbones among 4 plates. Add 2 toasts and 1 teaspoon of the remaining salt to each plate. Serve at once, accompanied by freshly ground pepper and the remaining 8 toasts. Diners can spread the bone marrow on their toasts, seasoning with pepper and salt as desired.

SERVES 4

8 beef marrowbones, each about 4 inches (10 cm) long, halved lengthwise by your butcher

1 bunch young purslane

2 small shallots, thinly sliced

2 Tbsp extra-virgin olive oil

1 Tbsp capers, rinsed and chopped

1 tsp fresh lemon juice

4¼ tsp coarse sea salt, preferably *sel de Guérande* (page 271)

¼ tsp freshly ground pepper, plus pepper for serving

16 slices baguette, grilled or toasted

PICKLED WILD MUSHROOMS

One of the ways my neighbors in France preserve a good season of wild mushrooms is by pickling them, especially the meaty sanguins and cèpes. Morels are also good candidates. Meaty cultivated mushrooms, such as king trumpet, oyster, and portobello, are amenable to pickling, as well. The pickled mushrooms, which can also be found at some traiteurs, or "delicatessens," and butcher shops, are then served throughout the winter and early spring as an accompaniment to aperitifs or as part of an appetizer platter along with olives and charcuterie.

Wash a 1-pt (16–fl oz/500-ml) canning jar and its lid in hot, soapy water, dry well, and set aside. Trim the mushroom stem ends, but leave the stems intact if they are firm and meaty. If not, remove and discard or save for broth (page 203). Slice the mushrooms lengthwise into ¼-inch (6-mm) slices or cut them into quarters.

In a nonreactive saucepan, combine ¼ cup (2 fl oz/65 ml) of the oil, ¼ cup (2 fl oz/65 ml) of the vinegar, the peppercorns, salt, and thyme and bring to a boil over medium-high heat. Boil for 2 minutes, then add the mushrooms, reduce the heat to low, and cook for exactly 2 minutes, turning the mushrooms constantly.

Ladle the mushrooms and hot liquid into the jar. Add the remaining ¼ cup (2 fl oz/60 ml) oil and ¼ cup (2 fl oz/60 ml) vinegar. Cover the jar loosely with aluminum foil and let cool to room temperature. Discard the foil and seal the jar. Refrigerate for at least 24 hours to allow the flavors to blend before serving. The oil will solidify somewhat but will liquefy again at room temperature. The mushrooms will keep in the refrigerator for up to 3 months.

Before serving, bring to room temperature. Serve as an hors d'oeuvre with toothpicks.

MAKES 1 PINT
(16 FL OZ/500 ML)

½ lb (250 g) firm mushrooms
½ cup (4 fl oz/125 ml) extra-virgin olive oil
½ cup (4 fl oz/125 ml) red wine vinegar
½ tsp black peppercorns
¼ tsp sea salt
14 fresh thyme sprigs

SNAIL-STUFFED MUSHROOMS

This is my version of a dish that I was served at a chambre d'hôte *housed in the eleventh-century Château de Volan, not far from Lyons. Valérie Seneclauze lives there with her family and cultivates shiitake mushrooms in the château's old wine caves. She explained that there were many food artisans in the region, and that for dinner that night we would be sampling her mushrooms paired with snails from a local farm.*

Place the 4 mushroom caps, gill side up, in a small baking dish. In a small bowl, stir together the oil, wine, salt, pepper, bay leaves, and thyme and pour evenly over the mushrooms. Let marinate at room temperature for 4 hours.

Preheat the oven to 400°F (200°C).

To make the filling, drain and rinse the snails and pat dry. Coarsely chop 20 of them and leave the remaining 16 whole. Finely chop the ½ lb (250 g) mushrooms and the reserved stems.

In a frying pan, melt 3 tablespoons of the butter with the oil over medium-high heat. Add the shallot and sauté until soft, about 1 minute. Add the mushrooms and stems and sauté until they release their juices, 4–5 minutes. Add the chopped and whole snails, thyme, salt, and pepper and cook, stirring, until the pan juices are reduced to about 2 tablespoons, 1–2 minutes.

With a slotted spoon, transfer the mushrooms and snails to a small bowl. Raise the heat to high, add the wine, and deglaze the pan by scraping up any bits that cling to the bottom. Reduce the heat to low and stir in the remaining 1 tablespoon butter and the mushrooms and snails with any collected juices. Cook just until the butter melts, about 1 minute. Stir well and set aside.

Place the marinated mushrooms in a single layer, gill side down, in the baking dish, and bake until softened and the caps begin to shrink, 10–12 minutes. Turn the mushrooms gill side up and distribute the snail mixture evenly among them. Continue to bake until the mushrooms are easily pierced with a fork, about 12 minutes. Garnish with the crème fraîche, if desired, and serve.

SERVES 4 AS
AN APPETIZER

4 shiitake mushrooms, brushed clean and trimmed, stems reserved

⅓ cup (3 fl oz/80 ml) extra-virgin olive oil

1 Tbsp dry red wine

½ tsp sea salt

½ tsp freshly ground pepper

2 fresh or 1 dried bay leaf

1 tsp minced fresh thyme

for the filling

36 canned large snails

½ lb (250 g) shiitake mushrooms, brushed clean

4 Tbsp (2 oz/60 g) unsalted butter

1 Tbsp extra-virgin olive oil

1 shallot, minced

1 tsp minced fresh thyme

½ tsp sea salt

¼ tsp freshly ground pepper

2 Tbsp dry red wine

¼ cup (2 fl oz/60 ml) crème fraîche (optional)

A SNAIL STORY

The earliest evidence of snail eating in Provence dates back more than twelve thousand years. The remains of ashes and snail shells, indicating the snails were cooked in coals, have been found in the aprons (flat areas at the entrances of prehistoric caves) in the region of Alpes-de-Haute-Provence, dating to at least 11,000 BCE. Archaeologists have unearthed several sites where such an impressive number of snail shells have been found that the sites are referred to as Mesolithic *escargotières*, or "snail farms."

The people of Provence have continued the tradition of cooking snails in coals, as well as developing more elegant culinary expressions. I have been told that up until the 1950s and 1960s, it was common to cook snails for lunch while working in the vineyards. The workers would build a fire of grapevine prunings in a clearing and place a rack over the coals to hold the snails, just the way their grandparents and great-grandparents did. The snails were picked from their shells with a pin or a needle and ideally would have been eaten with aioli alongside, still a popular combination in the region. In Marseilles, snail vendors plied their wares in the streets well into the 1930s, selling paper cones of cooked snails accompanied by a pick.

In my early years in Provence, my neighbors still gathered snails and cooked them, and so I learned to do it as well. After the rains, we scoured the roadsides and orchards and filled our buckets with plump snails. Some were the big ones, known as Burgundy snails, but most of them were the smaller snails known as *petit gris*. Once captured, we would put them in wooden grape-picking crates and put a lot of fresh thyme and wheat bran inside for them to feed on. Next, we fastened a wire-mesh screen snugly atop each crate. We kept an eye on the snails for two weeks while their systems were cleansed by eating the thyme and bran.

Before cooking them, one more step was required. The snails were removed to a bowl and carried into the kitchen. As I watched my neighbor Marie, she added roughly a cup (8 oz/250 g) of coarse salt per pound (500 g) of snails, covered the bowl with pinpricked aluminum foil, and let them stand overnight. The next day we cooked them in tomato sauce and ate them the traditional way, *à la sucerelle*, with our fingers, sucking the snails from their shells.

If you choose to raise your own snails, you can even buy special commercial snail food for your enterprise. While driving around the back roads of France, note the Élevage d'Escargots signs. If you follow the arrow, you'll no doubt have the opportunity to purchase live snails, purged and ready to cook, as well as a selection of canned and jarred snails in a variety of sauces.

TRUFFLED GOUGÈRES

Truffles are the most highly valued fungi in the world. The black truffle of France, known as the Périgord truffle, is pebbled and rough on the outside, grayish beige inside, and lightly veined with white. Its aroma is unlike anything else —earthy and foresty, with a lingering scent of an age-old underground world. With luck, you'll be friends with a truffle hunter who will give you a few —or at least sell them to you at a good price. Here in America, fine grocers are likely to have them, or you can special order them. I've tried, when I've had an ounce or so of truffle, to stretch it as far as possible. But I've learned it's better to just immerse oneself in the indulgence. A truffle's aroma and flavor are brought out by warmth; a warm puffy gougère *makes just the right carrier.*

Preheat the oven to 425°F (220°C).

In a saucepan, combine ½ cup (4 fl oz/125 ml) water, the butter, salt, white pepper, and cayenne. Bring to a boil over medium-high heat and cook, stirring, until the butter melts, 3–4 minutes. Add the flour all at once and stir vigorously with a wooden spoon until a thick paste forms and pulls away from the sides of the pan, about 3 minutes. Remove from the heat and make a well in the center of the paste. Crack 1 egg into the well and beat it into the hot paste, either with the wooden spoon or a whisk. Repeat with 1 more egg and beat until a smooth, sticky batter forms. Reserve the remaining egg.

Line a baking sheet with parchment paper. Have ready a teaspoon and a glass of hot water. To shape each *gougère*, dip the spoon into the water, scoop up a generous teaspoon of the mixture, and push it onto the baking sheet with your fingertips. Repeat, spacing the *gougères* about 1 inch (2.5 cm) apart and dipping the spoon in the cold water each time to prevent the dough from sticking.

In a small bowl, stir together the remaining 1 egg and 1 tablespoon water to make an egg wash. Using a pastry brush, brush the tops of the *gougères* with the egg wash, being careful not to let it drip onto the parchment.

MAKES ABOUT 16.
SERVES 4 AS AN
APPETIZER

3 Tbsp unsalted butter

½ tsp salt

¼ tsp freshly ground white pepper

⅛ tsp cayenne pepper

½ cup (2½ oz/75 g) all-purpose flour

3 large eggs

1½ oz (45 g) fresh black truffle (1–2 truffles)

Bake for 10 minutes, then reduce the heat to 350°F (180°C) and continue to bake until the *gougères* are golden brown and crunchy, about 15 minutes longer. If underdone, they will be mushy and uncooked inside. When done, pierce each *gougère* with a thin wooden skewer, then turn off the oven. Leave the *gougères* in the oven for 10 minutes.

Meanwhile, clean the truffle: Gently rinse with water and pat dry. Brush away any dirt with a small brush. I use a toothbrush reserved for that purpose. For a refined finish, you can closely scrape the rough outer skin with a paring knife, but it is not necessary. If you do scrape the skin, reserve it to make truffle oil (see below). Cut the truffle into the thinnest slices possible.

When ready to serve, remove the *gougères* from the oven and slice the still-warm *gougères* almost in half crosswise. Tuck a slice or two of truffle into each one and serve at once.

HOMEMADE TRUFFLE OIL

If you have saved the truffle scrapings from a recipe, or if you simply want to use a fresh truffle to make your own oil, this is an easy way to do it. Fill a ½-pt (8–fl oz/250-ml) jar with good-quality extra-virgin olive oil or grapeseed oil and add 2 teaspoons grated fresh truffle or truffle scrapings reserved from cleaning the truffles, or a combination. Seal the jar and put it in a cool, dark place for a week to allow the oil to become infused with the truffle, which will occur after several days. Keep the jar in a cool, dark place and use the oil to flavor soups or potatoes, or to make a vinaigrette, with mostly truffle oil and a little Champagne vinegar and salt, for a butterhead lettuce salad. The oil will keep for up to 2 months.

TRUFFLE WARS

Part of the allure of truffles is the mystery that surrounds them. For decades, they were sold surreptitiously out of burlap sacks, car trunks, and innocent-looking picnic baskets, trading directly from the truffle hunter's hands to the buyer's. Their value is significant—eight hundred dollars per pound (500 g)—so it's not surprising that truffle territory is closely guarded against poachers, those knowledgeable truffle hunters who steal the underground crop before its owners can get to it. Despite posted warnings, poaching continues.

A friend of mine, who has a hectare or so of truffle trees planted on his land near the Valensole plateau in the Alpes-de-Haute-Provence, went out one December morning with his dog to start harvesting his truffles, only to find the ground torn up and his crop gone.

Another friend, who leased truffle-hunting ground in one of the forests near his home in the upper Var, heard about poachers making raids in the area, invading leased lands and stealing the truffles in the night. That evening he staked himself out in a hunting blind on his property and waited. Not long after midnight, two men and two dogs appeared. The men were carrying large bags and moving stealthily toward the forest, letting their dogs loose to silently search out the scent of the truffles. My friend, who was big and burly with a notable temper, was enraged at the poachers' temerity. Leaping out from his hiding spot, yelling and screaming, he chased them and their dogs off the property. Word got around, as it does in small villages and rural areas, about what had happened to the poachers, and my friend had no more trouble—that season, anyway.

WILD MUSHROOM SOUP

It is pretty rewarding to come back from foraging for wild mushrooms with a basket of fungal loot. Chanterelles, hedgehogs, cèpes (porcini), black trumpets, puffballs — they are all good. The first night after foraging, I simply sauté them with olive oil, garlic, and parsley and serve them over toast. The second night, I make mushroom soup. Any mushrooms can be used for this soup. If fresh wild mushrooms aren't available, use cultivated ones, such as oyster, button, and portobello, with the addition of rehydrated dried cèpes to give the soup a taste of the wild.

In a large, heavy-bottomed saucepan or Dutch oven, melt the butter over medium heat. When it foams, add the shallot and sauté until soft, 2–3 minutes. Add 2¼ cups (6¾ oz/210 g) of the mushrooms (plus the rehydrated cèpes, if using cultivated mushrooms), the pepper, thyme, salt, and juniper berry and sauté until the mushrooms begin to soften, 3–4 minutes. With a slotted spoon, transfer the mushroom mixture to a bowl.

Raise the heat to medium-high, add the vermouth, and deglaze the pan by scraping up any bits that cling to the bottom. Boil until reduced by half, 1–2 minutes. Add the broth and ½ cup (8 fl oz/250 ml) water to the saucepan, along with the mushroom mixture and any collected juices. Reduce the heat to medium-low and cook, uncovered, until the mushrooms are soft and the flavors have blended, about 15 minutes. Whip the cream to soft peaks and gently stir it in.

Ladle the soup into bowls and garnish with the remaining ¼ cup (¾ oz/25 g) mushrooms. Serve at once.

SERVES 4–6

2 Tbsp unsalted butter

1 shallot, minced

2½ cups (7½ oz/235 g) finely chopped assorted fresh wild or cultivated mushrooms (from about ¾ lb/375 g), plus 6 slices dried cèpes, rehydrated and finely chopped, if using cultivated

1 tsp freshly ground pepper

½ tsp fresh thyme leaves

½ tsp sea salt

1 juniper berry, crushed

½ cup (4 fl oz/125 ml) dry vermouth, aromatic white wine such as Viognier or Roussanne, or dry white wine

3 cups (24 fl oz/750 ml) Mushroom Broth (facing page)

1 cup (8 fl oz/250 ml) heavy cream

MUSHROOM BROTH

Mushrooms make a full-flavored broth that can be used for Wild Mushroom Soup (at left) or any dish that calls for a vegetable broth. It can be made in advance and stored in an air-tight container in the freezer for up to 3 months.

In a heavy-bottomed soup pot or stockpot, combine the mushrooms, dried cèpes, carrots, leek, celery, cloves, salt, and 4 cups (32 fl oz/1 l) water. Bring to a boil over medium-high heat, cover, reduce the heat to low, and simmer until the vegetables have imparted their flavors to the broth, 45–60 minutes.

Remove from the heat. With a chinois or a fine-mesh sieve lined with cheesecloth, strain the broth and discard the solids. Use immediately, or cover and refrigerate the broth for up to 3 days or freeze for up to 3 months.

MAKES ABOUT
1 QUART
(32 FL OZ/1 L)

½ lb (250 g) fresh button or cremini mushrooms, brushed clean and coarsely chopped, including stems

6 slices dried cèpes

2 carrots, peeled and cut into 2-inch (5-cm) lengths

1 large leek, white and green parts, cut into 2-inch (5-cm) lengths

1 large rib celery, cut into 2-inch (5-cm) lengths

5 whole cloves

1 tsp sea salt

GRATIN of ESCARGOTS
à la BOURGUIGNON

Snails have been popular in France since before Roman times and the largest, Helix pomatia, *came to be called the Burgundy snail. The famous preparation of snails stuffed back into their shells after being cooked, then sealed in with lots of butter flavored with shallot, garlic, and parsley, takes its name from Burgundy, as well. However, snails are often served without their shells, in individual gratins or casseroles with various sauces. Good-quality canned snails are perfect for this and other escargot dishes, but it's fun to think of how in the old days they were gathered in the wild (page 197). Serve this with lots of bread for sopping up the sauce. Canned snails can be found in specialty markets or online. They come in various sizes and counts. In general, the larger the better.*

Preheat the oven to 400°F (200°C). Have ready four ½-cup (4–fl oz/125-ml) ramekins.

To prepare the snails, crumble the *pain de mie* into small pieces. In a small frying pan, melt the butter over medium-high heat. When it foams, add the bread pieces and toast, stirring, until golden, 2–3 minutes. Set aside.

Drain and rinse the snails and pat dry. Place them in a bowl with the wine, thyme, salt, and pepper. Stir several times and then let stand for 10 minutes.

To make the sauce, finely chop the parsley. With your hands, squeeze out the excess liquid. In a bowl, mix together the butter, parsley, garlic, salt, and pepper.

In a frying pan, melt the butter mixture over medium-high heat. When it has just melted, reduce the heat to medium, add the snails, without any collected juices, and cook, stirring, for 1–2 minutes. Stir in the crème fraîche and cook until slightly thickened and bright green, about 2 minutes. Taste and adjust the seasoning.

With a slotted spoon, transfer the snails to the ramekins, dividing them evenly. Pour the sauce over the snails and sprinkle with the toasted crumbs. Bake until the sauce is bubbling and a light golden crust has formed across the top, 10–12 minutes. Serve at once.

SERVES 4

for the snails

1 slice *pain de mie* or challah, crust removed

1 Tbsp unsalted butter

20–24 canned giant snails

¼ cup (2 fl oz/60 ml) dry white wine

1 tsp minced fresh thyme

¼ tsp each sea salt and freshly ground pepper

for the sauce

1 cup (1 oz/30 g) fresh flat-leaf parsley leaves (about ½ bunch)

7 Tbsp (3½ oz/105 g) unsalted butter, at room temperature

4 cloves garlic, minced

½ tsp sea salt

¼ tsp freshly ground pepper

5 Tbsp (3 fl oz/80 ml) crème fraîche

205.

FORAGED GREENS &
PROSCIUTTO SALAD

*The French countryside has numerous edible greens that are gathered in season, especially during the cooler weather of spring and fall. The tradition of using foraged greens for salads is an ancient one, but, as with so many old ways, the tradition is coming back into fashion. The flavors and textures of purslane, wild chicory, amaranth, and dandelion leaves, which are among the most common, bring a taste of the wild to the table. I like to combine them with silky slivers of salt-cured ham—*jambon cru *in France,* prosciutto *in Italy—for a salad that is both simple and special. Foraging is becoming increasingly popular today, and in many areas, both in the United States and Europe, there are foraging forays led by chefs, botanists, or both. As always, never eat something from the wild unless you are sure it is truly edible. A flavorful combination of cultivated greens, such as arugula, frisée, and dandelion, can be used to create a similar salad.*

In a salad bowl, whisk together the oil, vinegar, and salt.

Tear any large leaves of the greens into bite-size pieces, leaving small leaves whole. Add the torn and whole greens to the salad bowl and toss well to coat them with the dressing. Add all but a few of the prosciutto strips and toss again. Garnish with the remaining prosciutto and serve at once.

SERVES 4

3 Tbsp extra-virgin
olive oil

1 Tbsp red wine vinegar

¼ teaspoon sea salt

4 cups (4 oz/125 g) mixed
wild greens such
as amaranth, purslane,
and dandelion leaves,
coarse stems removed

2 oz (60 g) thinly sliced
prosciutto, cut into
½-inch (12-mm) strips

WILD FENNEL-GRILLED FISH

Wild fennel grows throughout the Mediterranean Basin and along the western coast of North America, including California, where it lines highways and roads. It even flourishes in urban settings wherever there is a bit of untended land. However, the more urban your setting, the more important to wash the wild fennel well before using. In Provence, wild fennel makes a popular bed for grilled fish, and that is how I've used it here. It blooms in early spring and summer with youthful, leafy stalks, and by fall, the stalks are as thick as a finger and crowned with flowering umbels of yellow blossoms. All of it can be used for cooking, including the pollen. If you don't have wild fennel in your area, use the stalks and fronds of cultivated fennel.

Prepare a charcoal or wood in a grill or preheat a gas grill. Rub the grill grates well with olive oil.

While the grill is warming up, remove the fish from the refrigerator and let stand at room temperature for 30 minutes. Pat dry inside and out.

Rub the fish all over with the oil and season with the salt and pepper, including inside the cavity. Break 1 of the fennel stalks in half and tuck it into the fish cavity, along with 4 of the lemon slices. If using fennel seeds, rub them all over the fish, including in the cavity. Place 2 of the fennel stalks in a fish grilling basket, if you have one, or directly on the grill grate at an angle. Lay the fish on top of the fennel stalks and cover with the remaining 2 fennel stalks.

Grill until the skin on the bottom is golden and crisp and easily separates from the grill basket or grill grate, about 8 minutes. If the skin is crisped, the fish is less likely to stick. If using a basket, simply flip it over. If you are cooking directly on the grill grate, slip a long spatula under the fish and place a second

continued on next page

SERVES 4

1 whole fish such as rock cod or sea bass, 3–3½ lb (1.5–1.75 kg), cleaned and scaled but with head and tail intact

2 Tbsp extra-virgin olive oil

2 tsp sea salt

1 tsp freshly ground pepper

5 wild fennel stalks, each 12–18 inches (30–45 cm) long, or 5 cultivated fennel stalks and fronds plus 2 tsp fennel seeds

2 lemons, thinly sliced

spatula on top to help flip it. Grill until the skin on the second side is crisp and golden and an instant-read thermometer inserted into the thickest part of the fish but not touching bone registers 135°F (57°C). When it's done, the flesh should flake easily when gently separated with the tip of a knife.

With the 2 spatulas, transfer the fish to a platter, using the same technique you used to flip the fish. Remove and discard the fennel stalks from the top and bottom of the fish and the fennel stalks and lemon slices from inside the cavity. Let the fish rest for 5 minutes. Have a serving platter ready.

With a sharp knife, cut the fish along the backbone from the head to the tail. Make a crosscut behind the head from one side to the other and a similar one behind the tail. With the flat of the knife parallel to the bone, gently lift the top fillet away from the bone and transfer to the serving platter. Starting from the tail, lift the bone until it separates from the bottom fillet. The head will remain attached to the bone, separating from the bottom fillet along with it. Discard the head, tail, and bone. Transfer the bottom fillet to the platter and garnish with the remaining lemon slices. Serve at once.

THE IMPORTANCE OF WILD FENNEL

More than once in France, I've been sent outside to bring back some stalks of wild fennel for grilling fish or for tripe stew. It is an important ingredient in bouillabaisse (page 264), and although cultivated fennel can be substituted, of course, it isn't quite the same as the wild variety. Even the seeds of the wild fennel, which are also used for bouillabaisse, are more intense than the cultivated ones. Wild fennel is a favorite for grilling fish—you make a bed of it on the grill (page 209)—and for flavoring *gras double* (page 220), sausages, and soups. Here in California, and in many other parts of the United States, it also grows wild. There's a big patch of it a few miles from my house along a freeway frontage road. In Provence, patches of it line my narrow country road. In fall, I collect the seeds and in summer the pollen, and I gather the stalks, both fresh and dried, year-round.

WILD MUSHROOM–STUFFED CHICKEN

This is one of my favorite dishes to make with wild mushrooms. It was inspired by a similar dish I had at Alain Ducasse's restaurant at La Bastide de Moustiers in Provence. The mushrooms are combined with sturdy homemade croutons, which keep their shape during cooking and absorb the flavor of the mushrooms without overpowering them, while the sauce gives another chance to show off the bounty of mushrooms. Although several steps are involved, this is not a complicated dish to make to celebrate the season.

Preheat the oven to 400°F (200°C).

Arrange the bread cubes in a single layer on a baking sheet. Bake, turning once, until toasted to a golden brown, about 15 minutes. Set aside. Reduce the oven to 350°F (180°C).

Trim just the tip of the mushroom stems, leaving the rest intact. Make the mushrooms look interesting by cutting some in half lengthwise, some into quarters, and leaving some whole, depending upon their size and shape. This is a dish that shows off the mushrooms, so they should be in large pieces.

Finely chop the giblets (liver, heart, and gizzard), or chop the chicken liver if the giblets are not included. Set aside.

In a frying pan, melt the butter over medium heat. When it foams, add two-thirds of the mushrooms, reserving the remaining mushrooms for the final sauce. Add the shallot and sprinkle with ½ teaspoon of the juniper, ½ teaspoon of the salt, and ¼ teaspoon of the pepper. Cook, stirring, until the mushrooms are cooked through and have begun to release their juices, about 5 minutes. Add ¼ cup (2 fl oz/60 ml) of the broth, then pour the contents of the frying pan into a bowl. Add the croutons, ½ teaspoon of the juniper, the parsley, thyme, and the chopped giblets or liver and stir until well combined. Set aside.

continued on next page

4-inch (10-cm) piece baguette, crust removed and cut into 1-inch (2.5-cm) cubes

¾ lb (375 g) assorted wild mushrooms such as chanterelles, cèpes, and black trumpets, or cultivated mushrooms such as oyster, portobello, and button

1 whole chicken, 4–4½ lb (2–2.25 kg), preferably with giblets

1 chicken liver, if giblets not included

2 Tbsp unsalted butter

2 Tbsp minced shallot

2 tsp crushed juniper berries

1 tsp sea salt

½ tsp freshly ground pepper

1 cup (8 fl oz/250 ml) chicken broth, homemade (page 166) or purchased

1 Tbsp minced fresh flat-leaf parsley

¼ tsp dried thyme

1 Tbsp brandy

Rub the chicken, inside and out, with the remaining ½ teaspoon salt and ¼ teaspoon pepper. Pack the cavity snugly with the stuffing to nearly overflowing. With kitchen string, tie the drumsticks together.

Place the stuffed chicken, breast side up, on a rack in a roasting pan just large enough to hold it. Roast, basting several times with the pan juices, until the skin is crispy and golden and the juice runs clear when a thigh is pierced with the tip of a knife, or an instant-read thermometer inserted into a thigh without touching the bone registers 165°F (74°C), about 1½ hours. Transfer the chicken to a carving board, loosely cover with aluminum foil, and let rest while you make the sauce.

To make the sauce, pour off all but 1 tablespoon of the juices from the roasting pan. Put the roasting pan over medium heat, add the reserved mushrooms, and cook just long enough to soften them, 2–3 minutes. With a slotted spoon, transfer the mushrooms to a bowl. Add ¼ cup (2 fl oz/60 ml) of the broth, the brandy, and the remaining 1 teaspoon juniper and deglaze the pan by scraping up any bits that cling to the bottom. Add the remaining ½ cup (4 fl oz/125 ml) broth and cook, stirring, until the liquid is reduced to about ½ cup (4 fl oz/125 ml), 1–2 minutes. Return the mushrooms to the sauce and turn off the heat. Cover and keep warm.

To carve the chicken, run a knife along one side of the breastbone, then cut across the base of the breast and along the sides to remove the whole half breast. Repeat on the other side. Cut each half breast in half again, being careful to keep the skin intact. Cut off the wings and drumsticks, then cut off the thighs.

Arrange the breast pieces in the middle of a platter and add the wings and thighs. Scoop the stuffing from the cavity and arrange it alongside the chicken, spooning some of the sauce over all. Serve at once, passing the remaining sauce on the side.

BRAISED PHEASANT, CABBAGE & CHANTERELLES

*I have various hunter friends who bring me pheasants, and this is the way
I like to prepare them. Pheasants are quite lean, so they need a bit of fat over
them to keep the meat moist while cooking. This could be thin layers of
fatback, pancetta, or bacon, which I use here. The fat not only bastes the
bird but also flavors the cabbage and mushrooms.*

Preheat the oven to 350°F (180°C). Have ready a large
Dutch oven or other heavy-bottomed ovenproof pot or dish
just large enough to hold the pheasants.

Pat the pheasants dry and rub them inside and out with
½ teaspoon of the pepper. Wrap them with the bacon by laying
3 slices across each breast and tucking the ends beneath the birds.

Sprinkle the garlic in the bottom of the Dutch oven and place
the pheasants on top of the garlic. Add 2 cups (16 fl oz/500 ml)
of the wine, the celery, thyme, rosemary, salt, and the remaining
½ teaspoon pepper. Cover and roast for about 35 minutes.
Uncover, tuck the cabbage wedges around the pheasants,
re-cover, and roast, adding a litte more wine if needed to keep
the cabbage moist, until the birds are tender and a leg easily
moves when grasped and turned, or an instant-read thermometer
inserted into the deepest part of the thigh without touching the
bone registers 165°F (74°C), 30–45 minutes longer. Uncover
during the last 15 minutes to allow the bacon and skin to brown.

Meanwhile, in a frying pan, melt the butter over medium-high
heat. When it foams, add the shallot and chanterelles and cook,
stirring, until the mushrooms are cooked through and have
begun to release their juices, about 5 minutes. Set aside.

Transfer the pheasants to a carving board and loosely cover
with aluminum foil. Remove and discard the celery and herbs
from the Dutch oven. Let stand for 10 minutes before carving.

continued on next page

SERVES 4

**2 pheasants, 2 lb (1 kg)
each, or 3 Cornish hens**

**1 tsp freshly
ground pepper**

**6 slices thin-cut bacon
or pancetta**

4 cloves garlic, minced

**2½ cups (20 fl oz/625 ml)
dry white wine**

**4 ribs celery, halved
crosswise**

6 fresh thyme sprigs

2 fresh rosemary sprigs

½ tsp sea salt

**1 small head green
cabbage, cut into 6 wedges**

3 Tbsp unsalted butter

1 shallot, minced

**½ lb (250 g) chanterelles,
brushed clean**

Heat the cabbage in the pot over medium heat, about 3 minutes. Add the chanterelles and any collected juices and stir for about 1 minute. Taste and adjust the seasoning, cover, and keep warm.

Remove the bacon and reserve half for serving. To carve the pheasants, run a knife along one side of the breastbone, then cut across the base of the breast and along the sides to remove the whole half breast. Repeat on the other side. Cut each half breast into slices. Cut off the wings and thighs with legs attached.

Using a slotted spoon, transfer the cabbage and mushrooms to a warmed platter and top with the pheasants. Boil the pan juices until reduced to about ½ cup (4 fl oz/125 ml), then pour the juices around the cabbage. Finely chop the reserved bacon, scatter over the pheasants and cabbage, and serve.

MUSHROOM-HUNTING ETIQUETTE

Is it okay to wander into the forest or along the roadside and gather mushrooms in France? Yes and no. If you see a sign posted at the entrance of a village or at the beginning of a forest's dirt trail or elsewhere that reads, *"Cueillette de champignons interdite sauf aux habitants de commune,"* you had best keep out if you are not a local. The signs mean that the hunting of mushrooms is a right reserved for the people living in the commune, or administrative district. Part of the reason for this is that wild mushrooms are an important economic resource for rural inhabitants, and outsiders coming in and taking them is like stealing part of their livelihood.

On the other hand, if you see no signs posted forbidding mushroom collecting or trespassing, it's probably fine to walk around and see what you can find. One strong caveat, however: never eat wild mushrooms unless they have been identified as edible by an expert. Trust me. In autumn when mushroom season begins in France, village pharmacies post mushroom posters and true-to-life

colored plaster casts of mushrooms in their windows. Anyone can take their fungal finds into the pharmacy, where they will be identified. If the pharmacist is a local, and most are, they'll no doubt inquire as to where you found the mushrooms. Everyone is always interested in where the wild mushrooms are flourishing, especially the highly valued cèpes, chanterelles, and *sanguins*.

In the United States, it's best to inquire about mushroom gathering on public lands, as there are often fees and regulations regarding amounts and designated areas. Private land is, well, private. I've found several edible types on my own property. I have friends in California whose backyards fill with cèpes, and others in the Midwest who have morels in their yards. The caveat, no matter where you are, remains the same: never eat wild mushrooms unless they have been identified as edible by an expert. In fecund mushroom areas of the United States, there will often be a mycological society that can help with identification.

WILD BOAR & CÈPE DAUBE

Wild boars flourish in many parts of France, and in some areas they have even become a serious pest, rooting in market gardens and vineyards, destroying crops. Over the decades, domestic pigs have escaped and mated with wild boars, creating a crossbreed that, like pigs, gives birth twice a year, greatly increasing the population. Fortunately, France is a nation of hunters, and they are delighted to pursue wild boars during the season. Wild boar occasionally appears on restaurant menus, but more often it is served in homes, usually in daubes, or stews, like this one. The key to success when cooking boar is the age of the animal. The meat of a young animal, which is typically lighter, will become tender more quickly than the darker meat of a boar several years old. You will need to taste the meat as it cooks to determine the doneness, allowing 1½ to 2 hours for a young boar and up to 4 hours for a more mature animal.

I like to serve this daube with boiled or mashed potatoes or wide egg noodles, a green salad, and a full-bodied red wine to match the rich flavor of the meat. In the absence of wild or farm-raised boar, pork shoulder can be substituted.

To make the marinade, cut the meat into 2½-inch (6-cm) cubes, trimming and discarding any large pieces of fat. Place the meat in a bowl. Add the carrots, onion, thyme, bay leaves, rosemary, garlic, juniper berries, salt, and peppercorns. Pour the wine over the top and turn several times to coat well. Cover and refrigerate overnight.

The next day, to assemble the daube, put the pancetta in a Dutch oven large enough to hold the boar mixture. Place the pot over medium-high heat. When the pot is hot, reduce the heat to low and cook until the fat renders and is at a depth of ¼ inch (6 mm), about 7 minutes. If there is not enough rendered fat, add a little lard. Discard the bits of pancetta.

Raise the heat to medium-high, add the onion and garlic, and sauté until the onion is translucent, 3–4 minutes. Using a slotted spoon, transfer the onion mixture to a plate. Remove the pot from the heat.

SERVES 6–8

for the marinade

4 lb (2 kg) boneless wild or farm-raised boar

3 carrots, peeled and cut into 1-inch (2.5-cm) pieces

1 yellow onion, quartered

8 fresh thyme sprigs

3 fresh or 2 dried bay leaves

2 fresh rosemary sprigs

2 cloves garlic, crushed

1 tsp juniper berries

1 tsp sea salt

1 tsp black peppercorns

1 (750-ml) bottle dry red wine such as Côtes du Rhône, Syrah, or Merlot

Using a slotted spoon, remove the meat from the marinade, reserving the marinade, and set aside on a platter lined with paper towels. Pat the meat with paper towels until it is very dry. Return the pot to medium-high heat. When the fat is hot, add the meat, a few pieces at time, and cook, turning several times, until well browned, about 4 minutes. Transfer the meat to a bowl. Repeat with the remaining boar. After the last batch of boar, sprinkle the flour over the fat and cook, stirring, just until it browns. Be careful not to burn the flour.

Raise the heat to high, slowly pour in the reserved marinade, including the herbs and vegetables, and deglaze the pot by scraping up any bits that cling to the bottom. Return the onion mixture and meat and any collected juices to the pot.

Add 1 cup (8 fl oz/250 ml) water, the parsley, salt, pepper, bay leaves, and orange zest and bring to a boil. Reduce the heat to low, cover, and simmer until the meat is tender enough to be cut with a fork, 1½–4 hours, depending on the age of the boar.

About 1 hour before the meat is done, rehydrate the dried cèpes in the boiling water, letting them stand for 30 minutes before draining through cheesecloth. Add the mushrooms and strained mushroom liquid to the stew during the last 30 minutes of cooking.

Remove from the heat. Discard the carrots and onions, or finely chop them and return them to the pot. Discard the herb sprigs, bay leaves, and orange zest. Skim the fat from the braising liquid and discard, if desired. Ladle the meat and vegetables into a serving dish. Serve at once.

for the daube

½ cup (4 oz/125) chopped pancetta

Lard, rendered duck fat or unsalted butter, and/or extra-virgin olive oil if needed

1 yellow onion, diced

2 cloves garlic, minced

2 Tbsp all-purpose flour

½ cup (¾ oz/20 g) chopped fresh flat-leaf parsley

1 tsp sea salt

½ tsp freshly ground pepper

2 fresh or 1 dried bay leaf

1 orange zest strip, about 4 inches (10 cm) long and 1 inch (2.5 cm) wide

2 oz (60 g) sliced dried cèpes

1 cup (8 fl oz/250 ml) boiling water

GRAS DOUBLE (PROVENÇAL TRIPE STEW)

As a young mother in Provence, I was enamored of my neighbor Marie's cooking. She could cook anything, and it was always unbelievably good. She used the vegetables from her potager, *the charcuterie she and her husband made every winter, fruit from their orchard, and rabbits and chickens from the hutches below the house. These were her basics, supplemented with pasta and with modest cuts of meat and inexpensive fish purchased from the traveling butcher and fishmonger who stopped on our country road each week. One day, Marie said she would make* gras double, *or "tripe stew," for me and ordered book tripe from the butcher for delivery the following Saturday. The next day, Sunday, she invited our family for lunch and served the rich, fennel-laced, tomato-flavored stew over boiled potatoes. We all had second servings, leaving just enough room for salad, the inevitable cheese course, and a fruit tart.*

The key to this dish is the tripe. Either honeycomb or book tripe (also known as leaf tripe) can be used, but it must be white, with no signs of yellow. It is typically sold blanched and parcooked, as is required for this recipe.

Fill a pot with just enough water to cover the tripe by about 1 inch (2.5 cm) and bring to a boil over medium-high heat. Meanwhile, rinse the tripe thoroughly in running cold water for several minutes.

When the water boils, add the vinegar and the tripe. Blanch the tripe for about 30 seconds and drain it into a colander. Rinse again under running cold water. Remove with tongs and cut into ½-inch (12-mm) squares. Set aside.

Over a sink, using your hands, squeeze out the seeds and extra juice from the tomatoes and discard. Chop the pulp. You should have about 5 cups (30 oz/940 g). Set aside.

In a Dutch oven or other large, heavy-bottomed pot, heat the oil over medium-high heat; there should be just enough

SERVES 6-8

3 lb (1.5 kg) blanched parcooked book or honeycomb tripe

¼ cup (2 fl oz/60 ml) white wine vinegar or distilled white vinegar

2 (28-oz/875-g) cans whole plum tomatoes, drained

¼ cup (2 fl oz/60 ml) extra-virgin olive oil, plus oil as needed

¼ lb (125 g) thick-cut bacon slices, cut crosswise into ½-inch (12-mm) pieces

oil to thinly coat the bottom. Add the bacon, onion, and garlic and sauté until the onion is soft and translucent, 3–5 minutes. Add 1 teaspoon of the salt, the pepper and the tomatoes. If needed, add a little more oil to prevent sticking. Cook, stirring, until the tomatoes begin to melt, about 10 minutes. Stir in the fennel, bay leaves, and sugar, then pour in 2 cups (16 fl oz/500 ml) water and the wine. Add the tripe and bring to just below a boil. Reduce the heat to low and simmer, adding up to 2 cups (16 fl oz/500 ml) water as needed to keep the tripe submerged, until the tripe is absolutely tender, 3–5 hours, depending on the maturity of the animal from which the tripe came. To taste for doneness, sample a piece. The sauce should be somewhat light and soupy. Taste and adjust the seasoning.

About 1 hour before the tripe is done, prepare the potatoes: Put the potatoes in a large pot, add water to cover by 2 inches (5 cm), and bring to a boil over high heat. Add the remaining 1 tablespoon salt, reduce the heat to medium, cover, and cook the potatoes until easily pierced with the tines of a fork, 30–40 minutes, depending upon their size. Drain and keep warm.

Just before serving, peel the still-warm potatoes with your fingers or a paring knife and put them in a serving bowl. Ladle the stew into bowls and let the diners add potatoes as desired. Serve at once.

3½ cups (14 oz/440 g) chopped white onion (from about 3 onions)

2 large cloves garlic, halved

1 tsp plus 1 Tbsp coarse sea salt

¾ tsp freshly ground pepper

1 stalk wild or cultivated fennel, about 4-inch (10-cm) long

3 fresh or 2 dried bay leaves

1 tsp sugar

2 cups (16 fl oz/500 ml) dry white wine

12 medium russet or yellow potatoes, unpeeled

QUAIL with JUNIPER GLAZE & SHALLOTS

Quail are smallish upland birds, with a mild flavor and firm flesh. They can be roasted whole or partially boned, with wings, legs, and thighs intact, and they make a casual yet impressive centerpiece for a dinner. I once attended a wedding where wood oven–roasted quail were served family-style on vintage platters at a long table. They were accompanied by roasted fall vegetables and salads of chicory and young lettuces. The affair was elegant in its simplicity, and we all felt comfortable finishing the birds with our fingers.

In a large bowl, combine the quail, pastis, 2 tablespoons of theoil, the sage, thyme, juniper berries, salt, pepper, and half of the shallot and turn several times to coat well. Cover and refrigerate overnight.

The next day, preheat the oven to 375°F (190°C).

Remove the quail from the marinade, allowing the excess marinade to drip back into the bowl. Reserve the marinade. Pat the quail dry. In a large ovenproof frying pan, heat the remaining 2 tablespoons oil over medium-high heat. When it is hot, add the quail and cook until the bottom side is golden, about 5 minutes. Flip them and cook until the second side is golden, about 5 minutes longer.

Transfer the frying pan to the oven and roast the quail until the juice runs clear at the deepest part of the thigh when pierced with the tip of a knife, 12–15 minutes if the quail are boned, 18–22 minutes if they are whole.

While the quail are roasting, prepare the glaze: Strain the marinade, pour into a small saucepan, add the remaining shallot, and bring to a boil over medium-high heat. Cook until reduced by half, about 5 minutes. Stir in the honey.

During the last 10 minutes of cooking, brush the quail several times with the glaze. When the quail are ready, remove from the oven, let rest for 5 minutes, and then, if desired, cut in half lengthwise. Arrange on a platter and serve.

SERVES 4

4 plump quail, about 1 lb (500 g) each, preferably partially boned

¼ cup (2 fl oz/60 ml) pastis

4 Tbsp (2 fl oz/60 ml) extra-virgin olive oil

3 fresh sage sprigs or 1 tsp dried sage

3 fresh thyme sprigs or 1 tsp dried thyme

10 juniper berries, crushed

2 tsp sea salt

2 tsp freshly ground pepper

¼ cup (1½ oz/45 g) minced shallot

2 tsp honey

FRESH BAY LEAVES SKEWERED
with EGGPLANT & PEPPERS

Sweet bay laurel, Laurus nobilis, *grows wild throughout the Mediterranean. Since ancient times, it has been used both dried and fresh. I have more than twenty sweet bay trees growing on my small farm here in California, and I use the leaves fresh all the time. They are intensely flavored and enhance everything from soups and stews to sauces and marinades. I realize not everyone has access to fresh bay, but should you have some, it contributes a smoky bay flavor to the meat and vegetables. If you don't have fresh bay, omit the bay from the skewers and add dried leaves to the marinade. You will need 6 metal or wooden skewers. If using wooden skewers, soak them in water for 30 minutes before loading them.*

In a bowl, combine the eggplant, lamb, onion, garlic, olive oil, and fresh or dried bay leaves. Sprinkle with the salt, pepper, and paprika. Turn several times to coat well and let marinate for 20 minutes.

To assemble a skewer, slide on a cube of eggplant, followed by a fresh bay leaf (if using), and then a cube of meat. Continue with the same order until you have 5 meat cubes. Repeat with the remaining skewers, eggplant, bay leaves, and meat, filling 6 skewers total.

Build a charcoal or wood fire in a grill or preheat a gas grill. Rub the grill grate well with grapeseed oil. When the grill is hot, grill the skewers until browning can be seen along the sides of the eggplant and meat, about 5 minutes. Flip and grill the other side for about 5 minutes longer. Check for doneness by pushing the meat with your finger. When it offers little or no resistance, it's done. Serve at once.

MAKES 6 SKEWERS;
SERVES 3-4

1½ lb (750 g) eggplant, cut into ½-inch (12-mm) cubes

1½ lb (750 g) boneless lamb shoulder or beef rib eye, cut into 1½-inch (4-cm) cubes (30 cubes)

¼ cup (1½ oz/45 g) minced yellow onion

2–3 cloves garlic, minced

1 Tbsp extra-virgin olive oil

24 fresh or 2 dried bay leaves

1 tsp sea salt

1 tsp freshly ground pepper

½ tsp sweet paprika

Grapeseed or canola oil for the grill

La Vie Rustic

MOREL MUSHROOMS
& STEAK à la CRÈME

In France, morel mushrooms are a favorite of home cooks and restaurant chefs alike. I'm an avid mushroom hunter, and I found my first morels not in France, but on the way to Soldier Creek in Modoc County in the far northeastern corner of California. Their distinctive cone-like shape covered with craters makes them hard to miss. You can also make this sauce with dried morels and any steak, or even ground sirloin, though beef tenderloin is the classic choice. I like to use rib eye, either boneless or bone in.

If using fresh morels, trim the tip of the stem end. Slice any large ones lengthwise in halves or quarters; leave smaller ones whole. Set aside. If using dried morels, rehydrate them in the boiling water, letting them stand for 30 minutes before draining through cheesecloth.

Pat the steaks dry and season them all over with ¾ teaspoon of the salt and ¼ teaspoon of the pepper. In a frying pan, heat 1 tablespoon of the butter and the oil over medium-high heat. When the pan is hot, sear the steaks for 1–2 minutes on each side for medium-rare. The surface will be browned and crusty. Transfer to a plate and cover loosely with aluminum foil to keep warm.

Pour off all but 1 tablespoon of the pan juices. Add the remaining 1 tablespoon butter to the pan and set over medium heat. Add the shallots, mushrooms, and the remaining ½ teaspoon salt and ¼ teaspoon pepper and cook, stirring, until the mushrooms are soft, 6–8 minutes if fresh or 8–11 minutes if dried. Add the crème fraîche and stir, without boiling, for 1–2 minutes. Continue to simmer, stirring, until a thin sauce forms, about 4 minutes. Gradually add the butter-flour mixture and stir until the sauce thickens.

Place the steaks on warmed plates, spoon the sauce and mushrooms over them, and serve at once.

SERVES 4

½ lb (250 g) fresh morels or ½ oz (15 g) dried morels

1 cup (8 fl oz/250 ml) boiling water, if using dried morels

4 boneless rib eye steaks, ½ inch (12 mm) thick, about 1½ lb (750 g) total

1¼ tsp sea salt

½ tsp freshly ground pepper

2 Tbsp unsalted butter

1 tsp extra-virgin olive oil

½ cup (3 oz/90 g) minced shallots

¾ cup plus 2 Tbsp (7 fl oz/220 ml) crème fraîche or heavy cream

1 Tbsp unsalted butter, at room temperature, mixed with 1 tsp all-purpose flour to make a paste

WINTER SAVORY ICE CREAM

Winter savory provides an intriguing, slightly resinous, woodsy background to this sweet, rich ice cream. I personally like it plain with sugar cookies, but for an extra fillip, brandy-soaked raisins and chopped toasted walnuts are tasty. Thyme is another herb that takes well to this simple infusion. I suggest making the ice cream mixture a day or two before you plan to serve the ice cream to allow the flavors to blend.

In a saucepan, heat the cream over medium-high heat to just below a boil. Add ½ cup (4 oz/125 g) of the sugar, stirring to combine, and then add the winter savory. Remove from the heat and let stand until the cream takes on the flavor of the winter savory, about 1 hour. Remove and discard the winter savory.

Put the egg yolks in a large bowl. Return the infused cream to medium-high heat and bring to just below a boil again. Whisk ½ cup (4 fl oz/125 ml) of the cream mixture into the egg yolks, then whisk the egg yolks, a little bit at a time, into the cream in the pan. Add the remaining ½ cup (4 oz/125 g) sugar and return the mixture to the heat, reducing the heat to medium. Cook, stirring, until the sugar has dissolved and the mixture has thickened and coats the back of the spoon, about 10 minutes. Pour the custard into a bowl and let cool to room temperature.

When the custard is cool, cover with plastic wrap and refrigerate for 12–24 hours.

Freeze in an ice-cream maker according to the manufacturer's instructions. To serve, scoop into bowls or glasses and garnish each serving with a winter savory sprig.

MAKES 1 QUART
(32 FL OZ/1 L)

4 cups (32 fl oz/1 l) heavy cream

1 cup (8 oz/250 g) sugar

10 fresh winter savory sprigs, plus sprigs for garnish

8 large egg yolks

SCENT OF THE GARRIGUE

When walking along the hillsides and trails of
Provence, the fragrance of the *garrigue* — the wild
scrubland that is a part of the Mediterranean
landscape — pervades with the scent of wild sage,
rosemary, juniper, lavender, and thyme. Another
scent of the *garrigue*, and my personal favorite, is
winter savory. More elusive, sharper leaved, and
darker green than its close look-alike, wild thyme,
it camouflages itself with other flattish, similar plants
that grow in the heavy, rocky soils, making it hard
to find simply by looking. Instead, I find it by touch
and by smell, breaking off pieces of the plants,
crushing the leaves between my fingers, seeking the
inimitable rush of peppery resin that signifies success
and gives truth to its colloquial name, *pebre d'âne*, or
"donkey pepper." This perennial, *sarriette* in French,
is an essential ingredient in herbes de Provence,
along with sage, rosemary, thyme, and sometimes
lavender. I use herbes de Provence to season
everything from pork chops to vegetables, but I
consider winter savory, on its own, to be the very
best seasoning for beans, both fresh and dried.

CRÈME BRÛLÉE with BLACK TRUFFLES

Sweet and earthy best describes this crème brûlée. The truffle slices warm beneath the hot brown sugar topping, which brings out their inimitable flavor.

Preheat the oven to 325°F (165°C). Have ready four ¾-cup (6–fl oz/180-ml) ramekins or gratin dishes and a broiler-proof baking dish just large enough to hold them.

In a large bowl, whisk together the egg yolks until thickened, about 2 minutes.

In a saucepan, combine the cream and granulated sugar and heat over medium-high heat, stirring until the sugar melts and small bubbles appear around the edges, 3–4 minutes. Remove from the heat, add the vanilla bean, and let stand. When the cream has a slight vanilla taste, after about 10 minutes, remove and discard the vanilla bean and strain the mixture through a chinois or fine-mesh sieve. Gradually whisk the cream mixture into the egg yolks and strain again.

Pour the custard into each of the ramekins, filling to within ¼ inch (6 mm) of the rim.

Bring a kettle of water to a boil over high heat. Place the ramekins in the baking dish and pour the boiling water into the dish to come halfway up the sides of the ramekins. Bake the custards until set but still a bit jiggly in the center and a thin, pale gold skin has formed on the top, 35–40 minutes.

continued on next page

SERVES 4

4 large egg yolks

2 cups (16 fl oz/500 ml) heavy cream

¼ cup (2 oz/60 g) granulated sugar

1-inch (2.5-cm) piece vanilla bean, split lengthwise

1½ oz (45 g) fresh black truffle (1–2 truffles)

3 Tbsp firmly packed brown sugar

Ice cubes

To clean the truffles, gently rinse them with water and thoroughly dry them. Brush away any dirt with a small brush. I use a toothbrush reserved for that purpose. For a refined finish, you can closely scrape the rough outer skin, but it is not necessary. If you do scrape the skin, reserve it to make truffle oil (page 199). Cut the truffles into the thinnest slices possible.

Transfer the baking dish to a wire rack and let the custards cool slightly. Remove the ramekins and let them cool to room temperature. Refrigerate until well chilled, at least 4 hours, or up to overnight.

When ready to serve, preheat the broiler. Layer the thin truffle slices over the top of each custard. Put the brown sugar into a fine-mesh sieve and, using a spoon, push it through the sieve, evenly sprinkling the tops of the custards. Return the ramekins to the baking dish, pour cold water around them to come halfway up their sides, and add several ice cubes to the water. Broil until the sugar melts and caramelizes, 2–3 minutes. Alternatively, caramelize the sugar with a small kitchen torch.

Transfer the custards to a wire rack and let cool until the surface hardens, about 10 minutes. Serve at once.

LAVENDER-PEPPER GOAT CHEESE

*Take a few stems of dried lavender (be sure they are pesticide-free) and rub them
together over a bowl. The flowers will shatter and release tiny black seeds that look
a bit like fine pepper, and in fact, lavender has a peppery taste. You can also add a
sprinkle of finely ground black pepper. Place a log or a round of fresh goat cheese on a
plate and sprinkle it with the crushed flowers and seeds, then drizzle it with some good
extra-virgin olive oil or honey and serve as an appetizer or as part of a cheese course.*

CHAPTER FIVE

THE WATER

THE WATER

FISH & SHELLFISH

FRANCE HAS MORE THAN 2,000 MILES (3,200 KM) OF COASTLINE ON THE ATLANTIC OCEAN AND THE MEDITERRANEAN SEA, SOME OF EUROPE'S MAJOR RIVERS, plus countless tributaries large and small, and many lakes. For centuries, the people along these coastlines and riverbanks have fed on some of the world's finest fish and shellfish as a matter of course. After all, they were there for the taking. I grew up in a small town in California on the Pacific Ocean, and we feasted on wild abalone and lobster when I was young, and later, I learned to fish, reeling in my own catch. It was simply part of life.

Bretons and Basques, Niçoise and Marseillais, and the others who dwell along the seas have developed countless ways to prepare their catches that speak to the *terroir*. Hence, you'll find Normandy lobsters with cream, Mediterranean mussels with pastis, and fish soups and stews with local vegetables and herbs. And just about any fish you can think of is grilled — with olive oil in the south and butter in the north. Fishing boats dock at small villages, where the day's catch is sold right off the boats. Restaurants often have their favorite, even designated, fisherman, and every cook knows the names of the local fish and how they should look and taste. Oysters arrive fresh and briny from the Atlantic coast, scallops are sold in their shells with their roe intact, and the little fish known as *petites fritures* arrive slippery and glistening, their eyes still bright. On the Mediterranean coast, the favorites are sardines and anchovies, which are grilled in great batches and eaten on the bone with one's hands, as well as spiny sea urchins. They all have annual festivals celebrating their gustatory virtues. More elegant than these humble sea creatures is the turbot, native to both the Mediterranean and the North Atlantic, a highly prized type of flounder that even has its own diamond-shaped cookware, a *turbotière*, usually made from copper—it's on my culinary wish list. Fish from the rivers and inland lakes and streams include pike, eel, shad, bream, zander,

trout, and perch. Lyon stands at the confluence of the Rhône and Saône Rivers, and its traditional dishes include *quenelles de brochet*, the ethereal fish dumplings made with pike, and *matelote*, eel cooked in red wine, which reflect the historical regional bounty. Grilled eel, one of my favorites, can be found on menus throughout the Loire Valley, along with grilled zander, sometimes cooked with potatoes in duck fat, a decadent accompaniment.

Crayfish are bountiful in freshwater, and one delicacy, Nantua sauce, a French classic, is made with whole crayfish, crushed and simmered, then strained. Crayfish are also used as garnishes for sauced fish dishes, not to mention crayfish boils, like those in the United States, where piles of the boiled crustaceans are peeled and eaten out of hand with butter.

SMOKED TROUT PÂTÉ

The French seem able to turn just about anything into a delectable spread, and this is the easiest one I know. Smoked salmon could be used instead of the trout, as could minced cooked shrimp or other shellfish. Serve this spread with toasts or crackers, or add a small spoonful to Belgian endive leaves as a special appetizer.

Break the trout into pieces and put in a bowl. Add the crème fraîche, the 1 tablespoon tarragon, the lemon zest, lemon juice, and pepper and mash together with a fork until a thick paste forms.

Pack the pâté into a crock or bowl and garnish with tarragon sprigs or a sprinkling of minced leaves. Serve at once or cover and refrigerate for up to 4 days.

MAKES ABOUT
1 CUP (6 ½ OZ / 200 G)

¼ lb (125 g)
smoked trout fillet

6 Tbsp (3 fl oz/90 ml)
crème fraîche

1 Tbsp minced fresh
tarragon, plus tarragon
sprigs or minced leaves
for garnish

½ tsp grated lemon zest

1 tsp fresh lemon juice

½ tsp freshly
ground pepper

GRILLED FRESH SARDINES or ANCHOVIES

Fresh sardines and anchovies are Mediterranean favorites, and there are even community feasts for sardines, called sardinards, *where hundreds of kilos of the fresh fish are grilled and brought to long community tables by the platterfuls to be eaten out of hand, never with fork or knife, or so says a Marseillais friend. I think in restaurants, however, knife and fork prevail. No matter how they are eaten, sardines or their smaller companion, anchovies, grilled until the skin crackles and chars and the flesh pulls back from the bone, make for a festive meal. In southeastern France, along the Mediterranean border with Spain, Banyuls vinegar, a specialty of the region, is served with the grilled fish, but elsewhere lemons are more common.*

Prepare a charcoal or wood fire in a grill or preheat a gas grill. Rub the grill grates well with grapeseed oil. Rub the outside of the fish with the olive oil, salt, and pepper.

When the grill is hot, place the fish in a grilling basket, if you have one, or directly on the grill grate at an angle. You may have to work in batches. Grill until the skin on the bottom crackles and separates from the grate without sticking, 4–5 minutes, depending on the size of the fish. If using a basket, simply flip it over. If you are cooking directly on the grill grate, flip the fish with a spatula and grill until the skin on the second side crackles and the flesh easily separates from the bone, 3–4 minutes longer. When the fish are cooked through, transfer them to a platter and loosely cover with aluminum foil. Repeat until all of the fish are cooked.

Serve at once, with the lemons or vinegar on the side for squeezing or sprinkling on the fish.

SERVES 4

Grapeseed oil
for the grill

24 fresh sardines,
about 6 inches (15 cm)
long, or 48 fresh
anchovies, cleaned
but with heads and
tails intact

¼ cup (2 fl oz/60 ml)
extra-virgin olive oil

1 tsp coarse sea salt

½ tsp freshly
ground pepper

3 lemons, quartered,
or Banyuls vinegar

MOULES GRATINÉES

Cooked mussels on the half shell topped with a garlicky bread crumb mixture and briefly baked make an especially impressive appetizer but are quite simple to prepare. They can even be assembled early in the day and refrigerated, then baked just before serving. This is an ideal dish to make with leftover mussels and reserved shells from Moules au Pastis (page 254) or any other mussels that have been cooked to render a broth.

Preheat the oven to 450°F (230°C).

In a bowl, combine the bread crumbs, tomato, mussel broth, parsley, thyme, garlic, salt, and pepper. Stir in the oil a little at a time, adding just enough to hold the ingredients together.

Place a mussel in each half shell and cover each with about 1 tablespoon of the bread crumb mixture, mounding it to the rim of the shell and packing it tightly. Place the filled shells on a rimmed baking sheet.

Bake until the filling is golden brown, 12–14 minutes. If the filling is still pale, turn on the broiler and slide the baking sheet under it for 1–2 minutes.

Transfer to a serving platter and let cool slightly. Serve hot, warm, or at room temperature.

SERVES 4 AS
AN APPETIZER

¾ cup (3 oz/90 g) fine
dried bread crumbs

1 small tomato, peeled,
seeded, and minced

24 cooked mussels
(page 254) with
½ cup (4 fl oz/125 ml)
of their broth

1½ Tbsp minced
fresh flat-leaf parsley

1 Tbsp minced
fresh thyme

2 cloves garlic, minced

½ tsp sea salt

¼ tsp freshly
ground pepper

About 1 Tbsp
extra-virgin olive oil

24 mussel shell halves

PLATEAU de FRUITS de MER with MIGNONETTE SAUCE

This is my version of the Grand Royale served at the Terminus Nord Brasserie in Paris—an extravagant assortment of oysters, langoustine, crab, lobster, and whelks—accompanied with a classic mignonette, lemon quarters, and crusty bread and rich butter, and washed down with a crisp Muscadet from the Loire. At home, my seafood platters are not quite as grand, though the shellfish is always perfectly fresh.

To make the mignonette sauce, in a small bowl, stir together all of the ingredients. Cover and refrigerate for up to 24 hours.

Select the shellfish that appeals to you. You can purchase live crab and lobster and cook them (pages 270 and 273, respectively), or buy them already cooked. The same is true of shrimp, which are easily cooked by plunging them in boiling water until they are opaque, about 2 minutes, depending upon their size. Shuck the oysters (page 258) and clams and serve them on the half shell, or serve the clams with the shells open but hinges intact.

Cover a large serving platter with the ice and arrange the shellfish on it. Accompany with the mignonette sauce, chilled or at room temperature, and the lemon quarters.

SERVES 6

for the mignonette sauce

1½ cups (12 fl oz/375 ml) Champagne vinegar

6 Tbsp minced shallots

2 Tbsp cracked black pepper

¾ tsp sea salt

for the fruits de mer

Shellfish such as crab, lobster, shrimp, oysters, and clams

Crushed ice for serving

1 lemon, quartered

VIOLET DE ROCHE: AN APHRODISIAC?

Oysters have long been considered an aphrodisiac, but the Provençaux of old have their own aphrodisiac, the shellfish known as *violet de mer* (*Microcosmus sabatieri*), or *violet de roche* to differentiate it from the less tasty *violet de sable*. It's also called the sea fig because of its deep brownish purple color, or sea potato because of its lumpy potato shape. It's found in the shallow waters of the Mediterranean from Sète to Toulon, clamped onto rocks. *Violets de roche* used to be quite plentiful, but today they are somewhat rare, though highly sought after,

especially around the winter holidays. You might find these strange-looking shellfish as part of a *plateau de fruits de mer* in Marseille or nearby, cut in half to expose their edible yellow-orange interior. The *violet de roche* has a strong iodine odor and is usually eaten with a squeeze of lemon or with vinegar and shallots. I first had it at a New Year's Eve party at a friend's home and found it too strong for my liking, but the other guests were delighted to have the specialty and made lots of jokes about its aphrodisiac qualities.

SALT COD BRANDADE

For centuries, salt cod has been a significant part of the diet in the Mediterranean, and France, Spain, and Italy all have their own versions of what the French call brandade de morue, or salt cod whipped with olive oil—sometimes with potatoes added—to make a creamy spread. This renowned spread, which is part of the traditional Provençal Christmas Eve dinner (page 126), is surprisingly popular with people who think they don't like salt cod, so be sure you make plenty.

Place the salt cod in a large bowl and add cold water to cover. Refrigerate for at least 18 hours, or up to 24 hours, changing the water 3 or 4 times.

Fill a frying pan with cold water and set over medium-high heat. Bring to just below a boil, add the salt cod, and gently poach it until it flakes easily with a fork, about 10 minutes. With a slotted spoon or spatula, transfer the salt cod to a plate. With a fork, flake the fish, discarding any bones.

In a small saucepan, warm the milk over medium-high heat. Meanwhile, in a heavy-bottomed saucepan, combine the flaked cod and ¼ cup (2 fl oz/60 ml) of the olive oil and cook over low heat. Transfer to a mortar or a large bowl and, using a pestle or wooden spoon, mash the cod into the oil until it is thoroughly blended. Slowly add the remaining ¼ cup (2 fl oz/60 ml) of olive oil and the warm milk, mashing constantly until the mixture becomes a smooth, spreadable paste, about 10 minutes. Put the warm brandade into a serving bowl and serve with the grilled toasts.

SERVES 4 AS
AN APPETIZER

1½ lb (750 g) boneless skinless salt cod fillet

1 cup (8 fl oz/250 ml) whole milk

½ cup (4 fl oz/125 ml) extra-virgin olive oil

16 slices baguette, grilled or toasted

HOMEMADE SALT COD

Here is a simple way to make an acceptable facsimile of salt cod. Line a plate with plastic wrap and top with a bed of sea salt ¼ inch (6 mm) thick. Place 1 lb (500 g) skinless black cod fillet on the salt bed, rub the sides of the cod with more salt, and then top with a ¼-inch (6-mm) layer of salt. Cover well with plastic wrap and refrigerate overnight. The next day, rinse the fish and gently poach it in milk with a bay leaf, turning once, until it flakes with a fork, about 10 minutes per 1 inch (2.5 cm) of thickness. Remove from the liquid and use in any dish calling for salt cod.

CRAYFISH BEIGNETS

Crayfish aren't easy to find in the market, but for those who know where to find them along lakes, rivers, and streams, it's easy to catch a hundred or more with just a few baited traps. The small size and delicate flavor make them good candidates for beignets, although it's hard to resist eating them straight out of their shell and dipped in warm butter. Cooked shrimp, crabmeat, or salt cod also make excellent beignets. These battered bites are perfect as an appetizer at aperitif time. Look for frozen cooked crayfish tails, also known as crawfish and crawdads, at fish markets and Asian markets.

Fill a large pot with water, add the 1 tablespoon salt, and bring to a boil over high heat. Drop in the live crayfish, if using, and boil until they turn bright red and their tails curl, about 2 minutes. Remove with a slotted spoon and let cool. If using cooked frozen tails, drop them into the boiling water for 45 seconds, then drain.

When the crayfish are cool enough to handle, remove the tails by cutting them where they join the body. Cut the carapace of the tail with kitchen scissors and remove the meat. Cut the tails in half and set aside. Discard the heads, claws, and shells or save for fish stock (page 260).

In a bowl, stir together the flour, ¾ cup (6 fl oz/180 ml) water, the olive oil, 1 teaspoon salt, and baking powder. Add the crayfish tails, green onions, parsley, and lemon juice and mix well.

Pour the grapeseed oil into a heavy-bottomed saucepan or a Dutch oven to a depth of about 4 inches (10 cm) and heat over medium-high heat until it reaches 375°F (190°C) on a deep-frying thermometer. Have ready a glass filled with cold water and a tablespoon.

Working in batches to avoid crowding, drop the crayfish mixture by the heaping tablespoonful into the hot oil, dipping the spoon into the cold water before each scoop. Fry the beignets until puffed and golden, 3–4 minutes. Using a slotted spoon, transfer the beignets to a paper towel–lined platter to drain and cover to keep warm. Repeat until all of the crayfish batter is used. Garnish with the lemon slices and serve.

SERVES 4

1 Tbsp plus 1 tsp sea salt

1 lb (500 g) live crayfish or ½ lb (250 g) cooked frozen crayfish tails

1 Tbsp sea salt

1 cup (5 oz/155 g) all-purpose flour

1 Tbsp extra-virgin olive oil

1 tsp baking powder

3 green onions, white and green parts, minced

1 Tbsp minced fresh flat-leaf parsley

1 tsp fresh lemon juice

Grapeseed or canola oil for deep-frying

1 lemon, sliced, for garnish

SEARED SCALLOPS &
ENDIVE à l'ORANGE

*Sweet scallops and tart citrus have a natural affinity, and here both the
endive and the scallops are paired with the flavor of oranges. This exquisite
dish was inspired by one I ate at La Mirande, a restaurant in Avignon.*

To prepare the endive, in a sauté pan, combine the endive,
¼ cup (2 fl oz/60 ml) water, the butter, sugar, lemon juice, salt,
and pepper and bring to a boil over medium-high heat. Reduce
the heat to low, cover, and simmer until tender, 5–7 minutes.
Using tongs, transfer the endives to a paper towel–lined platter
and arrange in a single layer. Set aside.

To make the sauce, in a small saucepan, bring the orange juice
to a boil over medium-high heat. Reduce the heat to medium, stir
in the cream and salt, and simmer, stirring, until thickened, about
5 minutes. Strain the sauce through a chinois or fine-mesh sieve.

Return the sauce to the pan, stir in the zest, and bring to a simmer
over medium-high heat. Simmer for 1–2 minutes, then whisk in
2 tablespoons of the butter and cook until melted. Add more butter
if desired. Cover and keep warm while you cook the scallops.

To prepare the scallops, pat them very dry with paper towels
and season with the salt and pepper. In a large frying pan, heat
the olive oil and butter over medium-high heat. When the pan
is nearly smoking, add the scallops in batches to avoid crowding.
Sear until a layer ¼ inch (6 mm) thick at the bottom of each
scallop is opaque and a golden crust has formed, 1–2 minutes.
Turn and repeat on the other side. Be careful not to overcook
the scallops; their center should still be translucent.

Divide the endives evenly among 4 plates. Top each serving
with 4 scallops and drizzle with the sauce. Serve at once.

SERVES 4

for the Belgian endive

4 heads Belgian endive,
quartered lengthwise
and cored

1 Tbsp unsalted butter

½ tsp sugar

¼ tsp fresh lemon juice

¼ tsp sea salt

⅛ tsp freshly
ground pepper

for the sauce

Juice of ½ orange

2 Tbsp heavy cream

⅛ tsp sea salt

1 Tbsp grated orange zest

2–3 Tbsp unsalted butter

for the scallops

16 sea scallops

1 tsp sea salt

½ tsp freshly
ground pepper

2 tsp extra-virgin olive oil

2 tsp unsalted butter

THIN-SLICED RAW SCALLOPS
with WILD FENNEL POLLEN

Scallops at their very best are like butter—smooth, yet firm—with a taste of brine. Thinly sliced, with a drizzle of extra-virgin olive oil, a pinch of coarse sea salt, and a bit of wild fennel pollen is the simplest expression of their quality that I know. For this super-simple dish, the only trick is to acquire sashimi-grade scallops, and they should be labeled "dry"—not "wet." Wet scallops have been chemically treated and contain excess liquid. If you are hesitant about eating raw scallops, lightly sear them first. You can collect wild fennel pollen by shaking a head of flowers into your hand. It will take several heads to make a teaspoon or so, but it is worth it. Fennel pollen can also be purchased at fine food stores or online.

Cut the scallops into paper-thin slices using a very sharp knife. Arrange the slices on a platter or individual plates in an over-lapping pattern. Drizzle with the oil and sprinkle with the salt and fennel pollen.

Cut a thin slice off both ends of the orange. Using a zester or a paring knife, remove the zest. (If you would like to garnish the scallops with orange zest, finely chop enough zest to measure 1 teaspoon and set aside.) Stand the orange upright and, using a paring knife, cut off the white membrane, cutting downward and following the contour of the fruit. Holding the fruit in your nondominant hand, carefully cut along either side of each section to release it from the membrane. You will need 12 small, thin sections, or supremes, about ¼ inch (6 mm) thick.

Garnish the platter or plates with the supremes, a few fennel sprigs, and the orange zest, if using. Serve at once.

SERVES 4

8 sea scallops, preferably dry, chilled
1 Tbsp extra-virgin oil
1 tsp coarse sea salt
4 tsp fennel pollen
1 blood or navel orange
Fennel frond sprigs for garnish

MOULES au PASTIS

A woman from Marseille first taught me to cook mussels. Good fresh mussels, garlic, and wine are the main ingredients. As the mussels open and release their briny juices, the broth is created. The mussels are cooked through as soon as they open, so don't overcook them, or they'll be tough. I've followed her basic rules ever since, and I've never been disappointed. Sometimes I'll add red pepper flakes or use a little pastis or change up the herbs, but the core principle remains the same. Serve the mussels with plenty of bread for sopping up the broth, which just may be my favorite part. I sometimes cook extra mussels if I want to make Moules Gratinées (page 245) the next day.

In a large stockpot, heat the oil and butter over medium-high heat. When they are hot, add the onion and sauté until translucent, about 2 minutes. Add the mussels and pour in the wine and the pastis. Rub the thyme sprigs between your hands over the pot, allowing the leaves to fall over the mussels, or add the 1 teaspoon leaves. Add the bay leaves and the fennel. Grate the garlic cloves directly over the mussels. Cover, reduce the heat to low, and cook just until the mussels open, 10–12 minutes.

Uncover and turn the mussels several times—most of them should be open. If not, cover and continue to cook for 1–2 minutes longer.

Remove and discard the fennel stalk, if using, and the bay leaves. Using a large slotted spoon, scoop the mussels into bowls, discarding any mussels that failed to open. Ladle a little broth into each bowl and serve at once.

If you are saving mussels to make Moules Gratinées the next day, remove them from their shells, put them in a bowl, and cover them with broth. Reserve some of the shells, as well. You can also shell mussels and store them in broth for a day for making a risotto or pasta.

SERVES 4

1 Tbsp extra-virgin olive oil

1 Tbsp unsalted butter

½ yellow onion, chopped

5 lb (2.5 kg) mussels, scrubbed and debearded if necessary

¾ cup (6 fl oz/180 ml) dry white wine

¼ cup (2 fl oz/60 ml) pastis

4 fresh thyme sprigs or 1 tsp fresh thyme leaves

2 fresh or 1 dried bay leaf

1 wild fennel stalk or ½ tsp fennel seeds

2–3 cloves garlic

PETITES FRITURES & AIOLI

Petites fritures, or "small fries," are the tiny anchovies and other small fish from the Mediterranean, only 2 inches (5 cm) or so long, that are fried in heaps and eaten whole, by hand or fork, along with lemon juice and sometimes aioli. My grandchildren find the little fish both fascinating and tasty; they always want to buy some from the fishmongers at the markets. They eat them one by one, leaving only the heads in a careful stack on the side of their plate. Here in California, I buy ocean smelt, which are a little longer, up to 3 inches (7.5 cm), but equally good.

To make the aioli, combine the grapeseed oil with ¼ cup (2 fl oz/60 ml) of the olive oil. In a small bowl, pound the garlic cloves and salt together with a pestle to form a paste and set aside. In a large bowl, whisk the egg yolks until blended. Add the oil mixture to the egg yolks, a drop at a time, and continue to whisk until the mixture emulsifies. If needed, whisk in up to 4 tablespoons more oil, a little bit at a time, until the mixture forms a mayonnaise-like consistency, adding only as much of the oil as needed. Gently stir in the garlic and salt mixture. Season with pepper. Cover and refrigerate until serving. You should have about 1 cup (8 fl oz/250 ml).

Pat the fish dry. Pour the grapeseed oil into a frying pan to a depth of 1 inch (2.5 cm) and heat the oil over medium-high heat until it reaches 375°F (190°C) on a deep-frying thermometer. In a bowl, whisk together the flour, salt, and pepper and transfer to a platter or a sheet of aluminum foil.

When the oil is hot, dredge a handful of fish in the flour mixture, turning to coat and shaking the excess flour through your fingers before carefully dropping them into the oil. Fry until golden, about 1 minute per side. With a spatula or slotted spoon, transfer to a paper towel–lined plate. Repeat with the remaining fish.

Sprinkle with a little salt, then serve at once with the aioli.

SERVES 4–6

for the aioli

¼ cup (2 fl oz/60 ml) grapeseed or other mild oil

¼ cup (2 fl oz/60 ml) extra-virgin olive oil, plus more as needed

3–5 cloves garlic

½ tsp coarse sea salt

3 large egg yolks, at room temperature

Freshly ground pepper

2 lb (1 kg) petites fritures or ocean smelt

Grapeseed or canola oil for frying

1 cup (5 oz/155 g) all-purpose flour

2 tsp coarse sea salt, plus salt for sprinkling

1 tsp freshly ground pepper

OYSTER CHOWDER

In this French-style chowder, some of the potatoes are puréed to form a creamy base for a quick poach of the oysters. The base can be made ahead, then gently reheated with the oysters shortly before you are ready to serve. Good-quality jarred oysters are perfectly suitable to use if fresh oysters aren't readily available.

To shuck the oysters, wrap a kitchen towel over your nondominant hand and use it to hold the oyster firmly, round side down. Using an oyster knife in the other hand, slip the tip of the knife inside the shell at the base of the oyster hinge, forcefully twist the knife, then lift up to open the hinge. Slide the knife blade under the top shell of the oyster to sever the muscle, then remove the top shell and slip the oyster and its liquor into a bowl. Discard the shell. If using large oysters, cut them in half. Set aside. If using jarred oysters, set the oysters and liquor aside.

In a heavy-bottomed saucepan or Dutch oven, melt the butter over medium heat. When it foams, add the celery, leek, shallot, and *jambon cru* and sauté until the vegetables soften, about 2 minutes. Raise the heat to high, add the wine, and deglaze the pan by scraping up any bits that cling to the bottom. Add the potatoes, 1½ cups (12 fl oz/375 ml) of the milk, and the oyster liquor and continue to cook until tiny bubbles appear around the edge of the milk. Reduce the heat to low, cover, and simmer until the potatoes can be pierced with the tip of a knife, about 30 minutes.

With an immersion or upright blender, purée about half of the chowder. Return the puréed chowder to the pan and stir to combine. Taste for salt—the liquor will have contributed some—and season with salt and the pepper. Add up to ½ cup (4 fl oz/125 ml) of the remaining milk for a slightly thinner chowder. Return the chowder to medium heat and continue to cook until tiny bubbles appear around the edge of the chowder. Taste and adjust the seasoning.

Add the oysters to the soup and poach just until their edges curl, about 2 minutes. Taste the soup and adjust the seasoning. Ladle the soup into a tureen or bowls and serve at once.

SERVES 4

12–14 small to medium oysters; 6 large oysters; or 1 jar (8 oz/250 g) small to medium oysters, with ½ cup (4 fl oz/125 ml) of the liquor (add water if needed)

2 Tbsp unsalted butter

2 ribs celery, minced

1 leek, white part only, minced

1 shallot, minced

1 thin slice *jambon cru* or prosciutto, chopped

¼ cup (2 fl oz/60 ml) dry white wine

2 russet or other starchy potatoes, peeled and cut into ½-inch (12-mm) cubes (about 2¼ cups/12 oz/375 g)

About 2 cups (16 fl oz/500 ml) whole milk

Sea salt

½ tsp freshly ground pepper

La Vie Rustic

POT de POISSON

This is a simple fish stew that's quick to make, especially if you have some frozen fish stock on hand, which I recommend (page 260). With a crisp green salad and plenty of bread, this makes a satisfying meal.

To make the broth, in a Dutch oven or other heavy-bottomed pot, bring the stock to a simmer over medium-high heat. Add the tomatoes and their juice, the thyme, salt, and pepper. Reduce the heat to medium and simmer until the flavors have blended, about 20 minutes.

To make the stew, remove and discard the thyme sprigs from the broth. Add the potato and celery and simmer until the potatoes are nearly tender when pierced with a fork, about 15 minutes. Taste and adjust the seasoning.

Add the fish and simmer until the fish almost flakes with a fork, about 4 minutes. Cut the sea scallops into quarters, if using. Add the shrimp and bay or sea scallops and continue to simmer until the fish flakes, the shrimp are pink, and the scallops are opaque, 1–2 minutes longer. Stir in the parsley.

Ladle the soup into bowls and serve at once.

SERVES 4

for the broth

8 cups (64 fl oz/2 l)
fish stock, homemade
(page 260) or purchased

2 cups (12 oz/375 g)
chopped tomatoes,
with their juice

2 fresh thyme sprigs

½ tsp sea salt

½ tsp freshly
ground pepper

for the stew

1 russet potato, peeled
and cut into ½-inch
(12-mm) pieces

½ cup (3 oz/90 g)
minced celery

1 lb (500 g) assorted
firm white fish fillets
such as halibut, sea bass,
and/or monkfish, cut into
1-inch (2.5-cm) cubes

½ lb (250 g) bay or
sea scallops, rinsed
and patted dry

½ lb (250 g) shrimp,
peeled and deveined

2 Tbsp minced fresh
flat-leaf parsley

SOUPE de POISSON with SPICY ROUILLE TOASTS

*This soup is the essence of seaside Provence in a spoonful, and it is my favorite
of all of the fish soups. Spooned over a rouille-topped grilled toast, it is usually
served as a first course, but I can eat several servings and call it a meal. This
recipe has multiple steps and you'll need a food mill, but none of it is complicated,
and it's well worth the effort. Be sure not to use any oily fish such as mackerel,
sardines, or tuna, as they are too strongly flavored for this soup.*

To make the stock, in a small stockpot, heat the oil over medium-high heat. Add the onion, garlic, carrots, and the white part of the leek and sauté until softened, 2–3 minutes. Add the fish parts and cook, stirring, until they begin to turn opaque, about 3 minutes. Add the leek greens, parsley, thyme, peppercorns, wine, and 6–8 cups (48–64 fl oz/1.5–2 l) water and bring to a boil, skimming off any foam that forms on the surface. Reduce the heat to low, cover, and simmer for about 30 minutes.

Remove from the heat. Using a slotted spoon, remove and discard the large solids, then strain the stock through a chinois or a fine-mesh sieve lined with cheesecloth. You should have 6–8 cups (48–64 fl oz/1.5–2 l); you will need 5 cups (40 fl oz/1.25 l) for this soup. Use the stock immediately, or let cool, cover, and refrigerate for up to 1 day or freeze for up to 3 months.

To make the rouille, use a mortar and pestle to grind the chiles to a powder. Add the garlic and salt and crush into a paste; the sharp edges of the coarse sea salt will act like little knives and help to make the paste. Add the bread crumbs and the saffron and its soaking water and continue to stir and crush the mixture with the pestle until a thick paste forms. Scrape the paste into a bowl, add the egg yolks, and whisk together until the mixture has thickened. Add ½ cup (4 fl oz/125 ml) of the oil, a drop at a time, and continue to whisk until the mixture emulsifies. If needed, add up to ¼ cup (2 fl oz/55 ml) more oil until the mixture forms a mayonnaise-like consistency, adding only as much of the oil as needed. Cover and refrigerate the rouille until serving.

SERVES 6

for the fish stock

2 Tbsp extra-virgin olive oil

1 large yellow onion, quartered lengthwise

2 cloves garlic, crushed

2 carrots, peeled and quartered crosswise

1 leek, white and green parts separated, then each cut into thirds crosswise

3 lb (1.5 kg) fish heads and frames from nonoily fish such as sea bass, snapper, or cod (gills removed)

4 fresh flat-leaf parsley sprigs

4 fresh thyme sprigs

8 black peppercorns

1½ cups (12 fl oz/375 ml) dry white wine

for the rouille

2 dried cayenne or other hot chiles, halved and seeded

6–8 cloves garlic, coarsely chopped

To make the soup, in a soup pot, heat the oil over medium heat. Add the fish, garlic, and onions and cook, stirring, until the fish begin to change color and turn opaque, about 5 minutes. Add the potatoes, bay leaves, and thyme and continue to cook, stirring to prevent any burning, about 5 minutes. Stir in the tomatoes, then add 2 cups (16 fl oz/500 ml) of the stock and deglaze the pan by scraping up any bits that cling to the bottom. Add the remaining 3 cups (24 fl oz/750 ml) stock, 1 cup (8 fl oz/250 ml) water, the fennel, salt, and pepper. Cover, reduce the heat to low, and cook until the potatoes are tender, about 30 minutes.

Position a food mill over a large bowl. Pour the contents of the soup pot into the mill and purée. Discard the solids in the mill. Rinse the mill thoroughly and purée the soup a second time, discarding the solids again. Transfer the puréed soup to a saucepan and set aside.

To prepare the toasts, preheat the oven to 400°F (200°C). Arrange the baguette slices on a baking sheet and drizzle with the oil. Bake until just barely golden, about 10 minutes. Turn and toast the second side until dried out, about 5 minutes. Remove the toasts from the oven and rub with the garlic.

Reheat the soup over medium heat until just below a boil, stirring constantly. Remove from the heat.

To serve, place a slice of toast in each of 6 soup bowls and dot each with a dollop of the rouille. Ladle the hot soup around the toast, just until it begins to float. Serve at once with the remaining toasts and rouille, ladling more soup into the bowls as desired.

Large pinch of coarse sea salt

2 large pinches of fresh bread crumbs

½ tsp saffron threads soaked in 1 Tbsp boiling water

2 large egg yolks, at room temperature

½–¾ cup (4–6 fl oz/125–180 ml) extra-virgin olive oil

for the soup

¼ cup (2 fl oz/60 ml) extra-virgin olive oil

1 lb (500 g) assorted whole small rockfish, cleaned and scaled but with heads and tails intact, gills removed

2 cloves garlic

2 yellow onions, quartered

4 russet potatoes, cut into ½-inch (12-mm) slices

2 fresh or 1 dried bay leaf

6 fresh thyme sprigs

6 large, very ripe tomatoes

4 wild or cultivated fennel stalks

½ tsp sea salt

½ tsp freshly ground pepper

for the toasts

1 baguette, cut on the diagonal into ¼-inch (6-mm) slices

2 Tbsp extra-virgin olive oil

2 cloves garlic

BOUILLABAISSE the MARSEILLE WAY

Marseille is famous for its bouillabaisse, but many other variations are found along the coast. Various versions of rouille, the spicy mayonnaise that accompanies the dish, exist as well. Here, the rouille incorporates bread crumbs for a very thick rendition of the sauce. Bouillabaisse, which is essentially fish and shellfish cooked in fish soup, is traditionally eaten in two courses. For the first course, a grilled toast topped with rouille is placed in each soup bowl and the soup is ladled on top. For the second course, the fish, shellfish, and boiled potatoes are arranged on a platter and moistened with a little soup. Use a variety of seafood, as that is part of the charm of the dish. Also, the custom is to use whole fish as well as fillets. If you are adept at filleting cooked fish, include a whole 2-pound (1 kg) fish in the mix, which will yield about half that weight in meat. If not, stay with the fillets.

To marinate the fish, arrange the fennel fronds and sliced fennel on a platter or baking sheet and lay the fish on top in a single layer. Sprinkle the fish with the saffron, pastis (if using), fennel seeds, and salt. Drizzle with the oil and turn several times to coat. Let stand at room temperature, loosely covered, for 2 hours.

To make the rouille, use a mortar and pestle to grind the chiles to a powder. Add the garlic and the salt and crush into a paste; the sharp edges of the coarse sea salt will act like little knives and help to make the paste. Add the bread crumbs and continue to stir and crush the mixture with the pestle until a paste forms. Scrape the paste into a bowl, add the egg yolks, and whisk together until the mixture has thickened. Add ½ cup (4 fl oz/125 ml) of the oil, a drop at a time, and continue to whisk until the mixture emulsifies. If needed, add up to about 3 tablespoons more oil until the mixture forms a mayonnaise-like consistency, adding only as much of the oil as needed. Cover and refrigerate the rouille until serving.

SERVES 8 GENEROUSLY

for the fish marinade

Fronds from 2 cultivated fennel bulbs or 6 wild fennel stalks and fronds

1 fennel bulb, thinly sliced

1 lb (500 g) halibut or monkfish fillets, about ¾ inch (2 cm) thick, cut into 1-inch (2.5-cm) chunks

½ lb (250 g) each of 4 different fish fillets such as sole, sea bass, red snapper, true cod, black cod, or rockfish (nonoily fish)

Pinch of saffron threads

2 Tbsp pastis or Pernod (optional)

1 tsp fennel seeds

½ tsp sea salt

¼ cup (2 fl oz/60 ml) extra-virgin olive oil

To prepare the toasts, preheat the oven to 400°F (200°C). Arrange the baguette slices on a baking sheet and drizzle with the oil. Bake until just golden, about 10 minutes. Turn and toast the second side until dry, about 5 minutes. Set aside.

To cook the potatoes, put them in a large stockpot and add water to cover by 3 inches (7.5 cm) and the salt. Bring to a boil over high heat, reduce the heat to medium, and cook until tender when pierced with a fork, 30–40 minutes. Drain, return to the pot, and cover to keep warm.

To finish, in a large, wide pot, bring the soupe de poisson to a boil over medium-high heat. Bring a kettle of water to a boil. When the soup is simmering, slide the halibut and any other thick pieces of fish across the top of the surface and push gently into the soup. Add up to ½ cup (4 fl oz/125 ml) boiling water to submerge the fish if needed. Cook for 6 minutes, then add the thinner fish fillets, pushing them gently into the soup. Again, add more boiling water if needed and cook just until opaque, about 4 minutes longer.

With a slotted spoon, gently transfer the cooked fish to a platter and cover loosely with aluminum foil to keep warm. Add the shrimp and mussels to the simmering soup and cook until the shrimp are opaque, about 2 minutes. Transfer the shrimp to the platter of fish and continue cooking the mussels just until they open, 5–7 minutes longer. Transfer the mussels to the platter, discarding any that failed to open. Bathe the platter of seafood with a ladleful of soup and cover loosely with foil to keep warm.

To serve, place a piece of toast in each of 8 soup bowls and dot each with a dollop of the rouille. Ladle ½–⅔ cup (4–5 fl oz/125–160 ml) soup into each bowl and serve at once, accompanied by the remaining toasts and rouille.

For the second course, arrange the fish and shellfish on a serving platter and surround them with the potatoes. Carry the platter to the table and serve some of each kind of seafood to each diner. Keep the soup warm over low heat for a second serving.

for the rouille

3 small dried hot chiles such as Thai chile, seeded and chopped

4 cloves garlic

½ tsp coarse sea salt

1½ Tbsp dried bread crumbs

3 large egg yolks

½ cup (4 fl oz/125 ml) extra-virgin olive oil, plus more as needed

for the toasts

1 baguette, cut on the diagonal into ¼-inch (6-mm) slices

1 Tbsp extra-virgin olive oil

for the potatoes

3 lb (1.5 kg) boiling potatoes, peeled

2 tsp sea salt

to finish

8 cups (64 fl oz/2 l) Soupe de Poisson (pages 260–261)

½ lb (250 g) shrimp, with heads and tails

1 lb (500 g) mussels, scrubbed and debearded if necessary

PANFRIED WHOLE TROUT with BROWN BUTTER & ALMONDS

There are still restaurants in France that keep live trout swimming in ponds or in enclosures built into the edges of rivers or lakes. Not far from my house in Provence, there is such a restaurant, once a relais, or "rest stop," for the stagecoaches that traveled over the mountains to the valleys and on to the coast. My daughter, Ethel, even at ten years old, loved to order the trout and became quite expert at filleting the fish. Trout are quite easy to cook, and the finish of toasted almonds and extra butter makes for a special, but not difficult, dish. Whole trout are often available boned, or you could substitute trout fillets.

Place the almonds in a small, dry frying pan and set over medium-high heat. Shake the pan continuously until the almonds become fragrant and turn a light brown, about 3 minutes. Pour onto a plate and set aside.

Rinse the trout, inside and out, and pat dry with paper towels.

In a large frying pan, melt 2 tablespoons of the butter over medium heat. (You may need to use 2 pans to accommodate the trout. Add half of the butter to each pan.) When it foams, add the trout, sprinkle with the salt and pepper, and cook until the skin on the bottom is golden and crisp, about 5 minutes. Turn and cook until the second side is golden and crisp and the flesh easily separates from the bone, about 4 minutes longer. Transfer to a platter and cover loosely with aluminum foil to keep warm.

Place the remaining 2 tablespoons butter in the pan and cook over medium-high heat, stirring, until the butter is lightly browned, about 3 minutes.

Pour the brown butter evenly over the fish and sprinkle with the toasted almonds. Serve at once with the lemon wedges.

SERVES 4

¼ cup (1¼ oz/35 g) slivered almonds

4 whole trout (about 1 lb/500 g each), cleaned and scaled but with heads and tails intact

4 Tbsp (2 oz/60 g) unsalted butter

½ tsp sea salt

½ tsp freshly ground pepper

Lemon wedges for garnish

266.

SEA BASS with LEMON VERBENA BEURRE BLANC

The Hotel Delos, built in the 1930s, is on the Île de Bendor, off the coast of Bandol. It is one of the so-called Pastis Islands because they were owned by Paul Ricard, of Ricard pastis fame. It's the kind of place that retains an untouched, simple glamour. The hotel has a restaurant with a seaside terrace. In the morning, you can see men in chef's whites getting ready for the day's meals, choosing the catch from local fishermen and bicycling with basketfuls of produce, just arrived on the ferry. I had the good fortune to stay and eat there one July. As part of the tasting menu, I had sea bass resting on a light, foamy sauce that was distinctly lemony but herbal, too. This is my version of the dish.

To make the sauce, in a small saucepan, heat the cream to just below a boil over medium-high heat. Add the lemon verbena and immediately remove from the heat. Let the cream and lemon verbena steep until the cream tastes of the herb, about 1 hour.

In a second small saucepan, bring the lemon juice and salt to a boil over medium heat. Reduce the heat to medium-low and stir in the infused cream, reserving the first saucepan. Simmer, stirring, until thickened, about 5 minutes. Strain the sauce through a chinois or fine-mesh sieve back into the reserved saucepan and discard the lemon verbena. Stir in the zest and bring to a simmer over medium-high heat. Simmer for 1–2 minutes, then whisk in the butter and cook until melted. Cover and keep warm while you cook the fish.

To prepare the fish, place it in a large bowl, sprinkle with the salt, pepper, and lemon juice, and turn several times to coat.

In a frying pan, heat the butter and oil over medium-high heat. Add the fish fillets and cook until the bottoms are golden and the fillets start to become opaque, about 5 minutes. Turn and cook until the second side is golden, about 4 minutes longer. The fish should be entirely opaque and easily flake with a fork.

Place each fish fillet on a plate or in a shallow bowl and drizzle the sauce over and around each fillet. Garnish with the lemon verbena leaves, if using, and serve at once.

SERVES 4

for the sauce

½ cup (4 fl oz/125 ml) heavy cream

10 fresh lemon verbena sprigs or ½ cup (½ oz/15 g) dried lemon verbena, plus 8 fresh leaves for garnish (optional)

1 Tbsp fresh lemon juice

⅛ tsp sea salt

1 tsp grated lemon zest

3 Tbsp unsalted butter

for the fish

4 sea bass fillets, each ¾–1 inch (2–2.5 cm) thick, 1¼–1½ lb (625–750 g) total

1 tsp sea salt

1 tsp freshly ground white or black pepper

1 Tbsp fresh lemon juice

1 Tbsp unsalted butter

1 Tbsp extra-virgin olive oil

FRESH COOKED CRAB with
SPICY MAYONNAISE SAUCE

*The best-tasting crab comes directly from the cooking pot. It is very easy to do.
Count on one crab per person for a generous feast, plus lemon slices or wedges.
And for my family, I make a spicy mayonnaise sauce. Sometimes I also use
the tomalley, the creamy yellow "crab butter" from the body, heating it slightly
with a little butter. My favorite wine with crab is Pinot Gris or a dry Riesling.*

Fill a large stockpot two-thirds full of water. Add the salt, lemon, and bay leaf and bring to a boil over high heat. Carefully drop the crabs into the water. Bring the water back to a boil and boil, uncovered, for 20 minutes.

Prepare an ice bath in a sink, tub, or large bowl or pot with a combination of ice cubes and cold water.

When the crabs are done, transfer them with tongs to the ice bath. Let stand for at least 10 minutes, or up to 30 minutes.

To clean the crabs, break off each leg by twisting it at the joint closest to the body. Set the legs aside. Place the crab rounded side down and, using the heels of your hands, press down on each side of the shell until it cracks down the middle. Pull off each half shell, then pry up the tail flap, pull it back, and twist it off. Turn the crab over and remove the spongy gills—the dead man's fingers—and discard. Leave the yellowish mass of crab butter intact for scooping out at the table, or scrape it out and discard it. (Crab butter is deliciously creamy and slightly bitter, which I like, but not everyone does.) Pinch the mouth and mandibles, pull off, and discard. Crack each segment of the legs and claws at the joint with a crab cracker, being careful not to crush the meat.

To make the spicy sauce, combine all of the ingredients in a bowl and stir to mix well. Taste and adjust the seasoning with more lemon juice or salt if needed. The sauce should be tangy.

Place the cracked crab in a bowl or on a platter and serve with lemon and, if desired, the spicy sauce.

SERVES 2–4

¼ cup (2 oz/60 g) sea salt

1 lemon, halved

1 fresh or ½ dried bay leaf

2 live crabs, each about 2 lb (1 kg)

for the spicy sauce (optional)

1½ cups (12 fl oz/375 ml) mayonnaise

3 sweet pickles, minced

3 Tbsp ketchup

Juice of 1 lemon

2 tsp Thai chile sauce

2 tsp sweet pickle juice

2 Tbsp minced shallot or yellow onion

¼ tsp cayenne pepper

¼ tsp sea salt

Lemon slices or wedges for garnish

SEL DE GUÉRANDE

Sel de Guérande is my favorite salt. Grayish and slightly moist, it seasons most of the food I cook. I buy the coarse type, *gros sel*, and grind it in a mortar with a pestle if I want it finer. The history of the Guérande saltworks fascinates me, and with every sprinkle, I feel part of a grand continuum.

The salt marshes of Guérande in Brittany have been harvested since the Iron Age, about three millennia ago. But in the late 1950s and early 1960s, they were being abandoned when sons were leaving the rude, severe life of a *paludier*, or salt worker, for better jobs in the shipyards in Saint-Nazaire and elsewhere, where salaries were higher and life less harsh. As the number of salt workers diminished, the salt ponds, long held by the same families, many for generations, were left untended. The sea began to reclaim the carefully planned complex of salt ponds first laid out by monks in the ninth century.

And then, after the protests of 1968, the back-to-the-land movement started in France. Young people, dismayed by the commercialization of life, became attracted to the traditional professions that were still practiced in the old ways, like sheepherding and the transhumance, making cheese by hand, and producing and harvesting salt from the sea.

In the case of the saltworks of Guérande, some young people who were raised there decided to return to carry on their family tradition. Others, who were raised in cities, learned the profession. They rented or bought pieces of the salt land, so they could practice the ancient trade and protect the fragile environment at the same time.

Today, there are three hundred *paludiers* in the Guérande region, and there is even a school where one can earn a certificate in salt farming, a program that takes two or three years. About two-thirds of the *paludiers* are members of the local cooperative, which was founded in the 1980s and handles worldwide sales and marketing.

The production area, which I visited a few years ago, was fascinating. It is essentially a network of basins, each protected by a raised earthen rim. Here, the seawater is directed, first into the outer basins, then successively into three more basins before reaching the last, the *oeillets*, where the water is fully evaporated by the wind and warm weather, leaving behind the coarse gray crystals of salt. When wind and weather allow, *fleur de sel*, considered the finest salt, can also be harvested as it forms light fluff on the surface of the water before the salt sinks to the bottom of the clay basins.

Once the water has evaporated, the salt workers rake up the pure salt and tarp it at the edge of the basins until it is ready to be delivered for packaging and shipping. The salt is given no other treatment.

Each basin produces between 2,000 and 8,000 pounds (900 and 3,600 kg) of salt each year or, in some years, none. About one month of warm, dry days is needed to harvest the salt, while the rest of the year is devoted to maintenance and to maintaining the flow of water through the network of canals and basins. A typical *paludier* will own or rent forty to sixty basins, for a total of 8 to 10 acres (3 to 4 hectares).

LOBSTER in SEAWEED SAUCE

The waters around France are home to many different kinds of seaweed, and fresh shellfish is often displayed with seaweed, served with seaweed, and in some places, Paris among them, you can purchase several varieties of it fresh. I've found that when fresh seaweed is not available, its taste can be captured in a sauce with dried seaweed, so here I have called for nori, which is commonly used for sushi. The lobster is parcooked, shelled, and then the meat is added to the sauce to finish. For a single serving, the claw meat is cut into several pieces and the tail is left whole. It can be served this way on its own or on top of pasta. If the lobster tails are cut into several pieces, two lobsters, with pasta, will serve four.

Prepare an ice bath in a sink, tub, or large bowl or pot with a combination of ice cubes and cold water.

Fill a large stockpot two-thirds full of water and bring to a boil over high heat. Using tongs, drop the lobsters headfirst into the water. Bring the water back to a boil and boil, uncovered, for 3½ minutes. Using the tongs, immediately transfer the lobsters to the ice bath. Let stand for at least 10 minutes, or up to 20 minutes. Transfer to a cutting board.

Using kitchen shears, cut off the claws and cut the carapace open. Remove the meat and set aside. Cut the tail from the body, then cut down the underside of the tail and remove the meat. Set aside. Cut the claws into ½-inch (12-mm) pieces and either cut the tail into pieces or leave it whole, depending on whether you are serving 2 or 4 people. Set aside. In a saucepan large enough to hold the lobsters' tail and claw shells, melt the butter over medium-high heat. Add half of the carrots, half of the celery, and half of the shallot and sauté, turning several times, until the vegetables are soft, 2–3 minutes. Add the tomato paste and cook, stirring, until it changes color slightly, about 2 minutes. Raise the heat to high

continued on next page

SERVES 2-4

2 live lobsters, each about 1¼ lb (625 g)

2 Tbsp unsalted butter

2 carrots, peeled and minced

2 ribs celery, minced

1 shallot, minced

2 Tbsp tomato paste

¼ cup (2 fl oz/60 ml) Calvados or dry white wine

1 sheet nori seaweed (about 7 by 8 inches/18 by 20 cm), plus 20 thin slivers for garnish

2 cups (16 fl oz/500 ml) fish stock, homemade (page 260) or purchased

¼ tsp freshly ground pepper

➡

and pour in the Calvados or wine. If using Calvados, light it with a match or igniter. Shake the pan until the flames dissipate, then break the nori sheet into pieces and add it to the pan along with the stock. Bring to a boil and add the pepper and lemon zest. Reduce the heat to medium-low and simmer, stirring occasionally, until slightly thickened, 15–20 minutes. Reduce the heat to low and simmer for about 10 minutes longer. Remove from the heat and strain through a chinois or fine-mesh sieve. Discard the solids.

Return the sauce to a clean saucepan and cook over medium-high heat until reduced to ¾ cup (6 fl oz/180 ml). In a small saucepan, heat ¼ cup (2 fl oz/60 ml) of the cream over medium heat. Gently whisk the warm cream into the sauce until well mixed. Taste and add up to ½ teaspoon salt, if desired. Set aside.

In a frying pan, heat the oil over medium-high heat. When it is hot, add the remaining shallot and sauté until softened, about 1 minute. Add the remaining carrot and sauté until slightly softened, about 1 minute longer. Add the remaining celery, stir, and then add the remaining 1 teaspoon cream and mix well. Set aside.

If serving pasta, bring a large pot of water to a boil over high heat. Add the salt and pasta, reduce the heat to medium, and cook until the pasta is al dente, 4–5 minutes. Using a wire skimmer, lift out the pasta nests, draining them well and keeping them intact. Place a nest in each of 2 or 4 shallow bowls.

If necessary, reheat the sauce over medium heat. When the sauce is hot, add the lobster meat from the tail and claws and turn them in the sauce until the meat is warmed through, about 2 minutes. If serving with pasta, using a slotted spoon, place the lobster atop the pasta, dividing it evenly. If not serving with pasta, divide the lobster between 2 plates. Spoon the sauce around the lobster, and then spoon a little of the sautéed shallot, carrot, and celery over the sauce. Garnish with the nori slivers and serve at once.

1 tsp grated lemon zest

¼ cup (2 fl oz/60 ml) plus 1 tsp cream

Sea salt (optional)

1½ Tbsp extra-virgin olive oil

for the pasta (optional)

2 tsp sea salt

2 or 4 angel-hair pasta nests

HOW TO EAT A SEA URCHIN

Spiny purple sea urchins were an important part of my Southern California childhood. When I would walk on rocks at the beach, I was always careful to avoid stepping on sea urchins because their spines really hurt my feet and the puncture wounds they made could get infected. It never occurred to my family—or to anyone I knew—that they were not only edible but also explosively briny and good. In Provence, friends told me about how they would go to the beach as children with their family, gather sea urchins, cut the shellfish open with a knife or scissors, and eat them on the spot.

I have since discovered a stainless-steel cutting tool, rather like odd-shaped scissors, made specifically for cutting open sea urchins in one crunch. Whether using the tool or kitchen scissors, be sure to wear gloves. Cradle the sea urchin, beak side up, in one hand. If using scissors, snip the shell open at the beak's hole and cut off the upper third of the shell, exposing the interior. The orange gonads are the edible part.

Pour off the liquid from the sea urchin and scrape out the darkish bits of the guts and discard them. You can now serve the sea urchin, with its edible orange sacs, directly from the shell, along with a wedge of lemon. Or scoop out the sacs with a spoon or a finger, rinse them briefly in salted water to rid them of dark bits, and arrange them on a platter or individual plates. Serve them with bread, butter, and lemon wedges, much as you would raw oysters. Sea urchins are best eaten fresh, but the gonads, often called roe or *uni,* can be refrigerated for up to 2 days.

SEA URCHIN SAUCE

Sea urchin sauce is a revelation in flavor. There is nothing to which I can compare it. It is briny, but crisp and clean and rich. This is a special sauce to serve over pasta (I love it on linguine), topped with some buttered bread crumbs and a sprinkle of freshly ground pepper and minced parsley. Look for the sea urchin roe, often labeled uni, *in fine seafood markets, Japanese markets, or online.*

To make the bread crumbs, tear the baguette slices into very small pieces, about the size of a pea. Melt the butter in a frying pan over medium-high heat. When it foams, add the bread crumbs and sauté until golden, about 5 minutes. Set aside.

To make the pasta, bring a large pot of salted water to a boil over high heat. Add the pasta, reduce the heat to medium, and cook until al dente, according to the package directions.

While the pasta is cooking, make the sauce: Combine the roe, butter, wine, and lemon juice in a blender and purée until smooth. Strain the sauce through a chinois or fine-mesh sieve. In a small saucepan, combine the roe mixture and cream and bring to a simmer over medium-high heat. Reduce the heat to low and simmer gently, stirring, until the sauce thickens slightly, 2–3 minutes. Taste and add the salt, if desired.

Drain the pasta and divide between 2 pasta bowls or plates. Spoon the hot sauce over the pasta, turning it a bit, then garnish with a sprinkle of pepper, the parsley, and the bread crumbs. Serve at once.

SERVES 2

for the bread crumbs

2 slices baguette, crusts removed

2 Tbsp unsalted butter

for the pasta

½ lb (250 g) dried pasta of your choice

for the sea urchin sauce

¼ lb (125 g) sea urchin roe (uni)

1 Tbsp unsalted butter

2 Tbsp dry white wine

1 tsp fresh lemon juice

2 Tbsp heavy cream

¼ tsp sea salt (optional)

Freshly ground pepper

1 Tbsp minced fresh flat-leaf parsley

A SIMPLE POTAGER WITH
FRUIT TREES FOR A SMALL PLACE

A *potager* will furnish your kitchen with fresh vegetables throughout the year. Its size depends upon your available space.

Once you have decided that you want a *potager* and that you have the basic elements necessary for one—sunlight, water, gardening ground or a place for containers—choosing what to plant, where to plant, and how much space to devote to it are mostly personal.

A classic *potager* contains herbs, annual vegetables, and a few cutting flowers. Ideally, it also has a few perennials, such as asparagus, artichokes, and strawberries. If you have more space, grapevines and one or two favorite fruit or nut trees can be planted at the edge.

Dwarf varieties of most fruit and nut trees are available and fit nicely into a small garden scheme. In "modern" *potagers* in France, it is not uncommon to find an espaliered dwarf apple tree or two between rows of vegetables. This is a break with the classic *potager*, which allows only berry fruits, not tree fruits, in the garden proper. Trees were traditionally planted only in the *verger*, or "orchard." But it is appealing to have a dwarf tree or two in the garden, especially since today most of us have limited space—and time—for gardening.

This simple 9-by-12-foot (2.75-by-3.7-m) seasonal *potager* plan includes herbs, salad greens, summer vegetables, and fall pumpkins

and will provide a family of four with fresh vegetables year-round in all but the most extreme climates. The garden can be started anytime of the year the ground can be worked. In other words, you can begin to plant when the earth is not frozen and a hard frost is not due for at least a couple of months. For example, you can launch your *potager* in spring with a first planting of peas, lettuces, carrots, and potatoes. Or it can be started in early summer with green bean seeds, tomato and pepper seedlings, summer squashes, pumpkins, and some zinnias. In late summer, lettuces, leeks, radishes, and turnips are good choices.

PREPARING THE GARDEN SITE

Regardless of which season you choose to start your garden, plan on allowing a sufficient period for ridding your site of currently growing weeds. You must also allot time for the weed seeds to germinate in the soil so you can remove them. The latter is especially important, for if you plant your garden with vegetable and flower seeds without first eliminating the existing weed seeds, your seeds and the weed seeds will germinate at the same time. Then you will have a great deal of work trying to free the tiny vegetable and flower seedlings that are intermixed with the weed seedlings. I have learned this the hard way, watching my beautiful rows of delicate lettuces being taken over by rapidly growing cheeseweeds, pig-weeds, and wild grasses, and I have saved them only by aggressive and repeated hoeing.

When the ground is soft enough, turn it over with a shovel or powered tiller to a depth of about 1 foot (30 cm) or so. Smooth the ground, breaking down any big clods and pulling out any weeds that are too large to turn over easily into the earth. Rake the site level and divide it into twelve squares, each roughly 3 feet (1 m) on a side. The plot should be three squares wide at the top and four squares long on the side. Plan on running two paths, each about 1 foot (30 cm) wide, between the rows, extending them the length of the plot. These paths allow you to reach all the parts of the garden without stepping on any plants.

Don't plant the garden now, no matter how much you want to begin. Instead, water it and watch for more weeds to sprout. When the weed seedlings are less than 2 inches (5 cm) high, hoe them again, cutting their roots and cultivating the soil. Rake again, this time mounding the soil of each square into a level bed about 6 inches (15 cm) high. Now you are ready to plant.

PLANTING THE GARDEN

The ground is ideal for planting when the weeds have just been removed and the soil is moist not far below the surface. Scratch down through the top inch (2.5 cm) of the soil to where it is damp and then plant your seeds into this moist layer. Press the soil firmly

back over the seeds to retain the moisture. You want enough dampness to germinate the seeds but not so much that the weed seeds will start again until you water the new seedlings in a week or so. By the time more weeds grow, your seedlings will have a good strong start.

Alternatively, plant your seeds in the ground 2 or 3 days after you cut down the second crop of weeds and water them immediately. Your seeds will still have a head start over the weeds, and your garden will be under way.

The *potager* is a rotational garden that is in an almost constant state of being seeded, cultivated, and harvested. While one season's harvest is in progress, another cleared garden space is being planted with the next season's seeds. The lists below note the vegetables and flowers that are best planted during a particular season. The plants that are marked with the symbol (*) are the easiest to grow.

SPRING

Spring vegetables need cool weather and water to grow and to remain tender. When the days become hot, the leafy vegetables become tough and the root vegetables become pithy and fibrous.

In early spring plant:

ARUGULA*, CARROTS, CHERVIL*, CHIVES*, DANDELION*, NASTURTIUMS*, LEEKS, LETTUCES*, PEAS, RADISHES*, SWEET PEAS*

In late spring plant:

BEETS, EGGPLANTS*, TOMATOES, ZUCCHINI

SUMMER

In summer, plants produce leafy or vining growths, but we eat the fruiting bodies. To produce mature fruits, the plants need warm soil, warm temperatures, and adequate water.

In early summer plant:

BASIL*, DILL*, MELONS*, PARSLEY, SHELL
BEANS*, SNAP BEANS*, SWEET PEPPERS

In midsummer plant:

BACHELOR BUTTONS, COSMOS*, FENNEL,
LEEKS, PUMPKINS*, RADICCHIO*,
SUNFLOWERS*, ZINNIAS*

FALL

The fall garden is planted in late summer
with seeds very much like those of spring.
Fall vegetables are leafy greens and young
roots, some of which will be harvested
quickly and others that will stay in place
over the winter, depending upon the climate.

In late summer or early fall plant:

ARUGULA*, CHARD, ESCAROLE*, FRISÉE*,
LETTUCE*, RADISHES*, SPINACH, TURNIPS*

Plant each of the garden squares with seeds
appropriate for the season, choosing from
the above lists. As you harvest one season's
crop—radishes, for example—plant your
garden square with seeds for the next
season. Many herbs are difficult to grow
from seed, especially the perennials (those
that return year after year), so they are
best planted as seedlings or cuttings. Buy
the perennial herbs listed below in small
pots or flats from a garden center and
transplant them into the garden anytime
of the year that weather permits:

MARJORAM, OREGANO, ROSEMARY,
SAGE, TARRAGON, THYME, WINTER SAVORY

Other herbs are readily grown from seed,
particularly annuals (those that must be

sown every year). Below are the most
common culinary herbs to grow from seed:

ARUGULA, BASIL, CHERVIL, CHIVES,
DILL, PARSLEY

ADDING PERENNIALS, BULBS, TUBERS & FRUIT TREES

If you want to plant perennials—asparagus,
artichokes, strawberries—consult your local
garden center for the best varieties for your
area and for the best time of the year to plant
them. If you have the space, potatoes, onions,
and garlic, which are grown from tubers and
bulbs, are all easy to cultivate. Place them
along the edges of your squares, or fill a
square or two with them instead of with
seasonal seeds or seedlings.

Most fruit trees are best planted bare root
when they are dormant. That means they
should go into the ground as soon as it can
be worked in late winter or early spring. As
noted earlier, consider dwarf varieties if space
is limited. Fruit trees can be planted anywhere
in your landscape—front yard, backyard, side
yard, even potted on a balcony or terrace—as
long as they receive at least a half day of full
sun. Ask your local garden center for the
best varieties for your area.

And finally, don't be afraid to fail. Prepare
the soil, plant the seeds or seedlings, water the
garden, and nature will take care of almost
everything except the weeding. Remember,
don't be discouraged if something doesn't grow.
All gardeners fail with a plant or seed or a garden scheme, usually several times each season.

Enjoy the *potager* for what it is—a daily
source of fresh vegetables and herbs grown
by you for your kitchen.

INDEX

ACKNOWLEDGEMENTS

I have written a number of cookbooks, so I am acutely aware that they reflect the efforts of many, many more people than just the author. I am especially grateful to the team that has collaborated to bring to life my stories and recipes for this large, dear-to-my-heart volume.

First of all, my deepest thanks to Amy Marr, associate publisher of Weldon Owen publishing, who, over lunch several years ago, first asked me what I would like to write. I told her about what would become *La Vie Rustic: Cooking & Living in the French Style*.

Without Michael Schwab and the Michael Schwab Studio, who created the rooster logo and the design for my product line, La Vie Rustic—Sustainable Living in the French Style, neither the line nor this book would exist. I cannot thank him enough. My thanks also to Carolyn Gibbs of Carolyn Gibbs Design—also the longtime assistant of Michael Schwab—who created the compelling presentation of what this book could be. And an extra thank you to both Michael and Carolyn for their whimsical illustrations throughout the book.

My sincere thanks to Hanh Le of Baytel Communications, who constructed the La Vie Rustic online store and taught me how to operate it.

Sara Remington, a photographer who knows and loves France—she even spent a week with me at my house in Provence—has beautifully and honestly captured the food and places in these pages. I'm endlessly appreciative of all of the work she has done to realize this volume.

Thank you to Ethel Brennan, my sweet and talented daughter. She is not only responsible for the thoughtful prop styling but also for conceptualizing and bringing to life on the pages the visions I sometimes have difficulty articulating.

I must also praise my gifted copy editors, Jane Tunks and Sharon Silva, who somehow keep my voice alive while excising the excess words. I cannot thank them enough for making whatever I write better.

There are many people to thank at Weldon Owen. Associate art director Lisa Berman had the challenging job of designing this complex book and has succeeded masterfully. Editors Lisa Atwood, Emma Rudolf, and Lesley Bruynesteyn kept everything on track, checking every teaspoon and regularly querying me about the smallest details—efforts I value highly. And a huge thank you to others at Weldon Owen, including Kelly Booth, creative director; Catherine Hebert, associate marketing manager; and Jamie Antoniou, senior publicity manager.

As a cook and a writer, I need and appreciate help in the kitchen. For this book, I had the assistance of a few indispensable people: Maribel Cervantes, who was a support throughout the project; Robert Thompson, who helped me realize the Lobster in Seaweed Sauce (page 273) and several other recipes; and Sam Petersen, who spent a weekend with me chopping, sautéing, and doing the dishes as I tested multiple recipes.

Every cook needs family and friends to share the food and table. And for this I thank my first husband, Donald Brennan; my son Oliver Brennan and his wife, Liz Valentine, and their children, Oona and Sidney; Ethel's husband—and my French son-in-law—Laurent, and their children, Oscar and Raphael; my son Tom and his wife, Katie Chapple Schrupp, and their children, Silas and Addie; and my son Dan and his wife, Stephanie Schrupp.

I've shared tables and kitchens with many friends over the years, and none longer than my friends and neighbors in Provence: Georgette and Denys Fine, Joanne Kauffman and Jim Gutenson, Adele and Pascal Degremont, Robert and Françoise Lamy, Marie and Marcel Palazolli, Anne Deregnaucourt, Maggie and Hubert Aupois, Nina Haag, Mark Haag. And now I am sharing them with their children and, in some instances, their grandchildren. All of them have taught me so much not only about food and France but also about friendship and community.

And last, but certainly not least, my heartfelt thanks to my dear husband and best friend of thirty years, Jim Schrupp. He has eaten, usually with great enthusiasm, everything I've ever cooked, and he has read every word I've ever written, with a keen eye and a love of language—and of me.

weldon**owen**

PRESIDENT & PUBLISHER	Roger Shaw
SVP, SALES & MARKETING	Amy Kaneko
FINANCE & OPERATIONS DIRECTOR	Philip Paulick
ASSOCIATE PUBLISHER	Amy Marr
SENIOR EDITOR	Lisa Atwood
ASSOCIATE EDITOR	Emma Rudolph
CREATIVE DIRECTOR	Kelly Booth
ASSOCIATE ART DIRECTOR	Lisa Berman
SENIOR PRODUCTION DESIGNER	Rachel Lopez Metzger
PRODUCTION DIRECTOR	Chris Hemesath
ASSOCIATE PRODUCTION DIRECTOR	Michelle Duggan
IMAGING MANAGER	Don Hill
PHOTOGRAPHER	Sara Remington
PRODUCTION FOOD STYLIST & PROP STYLIST	Ethel Brennan
LEAD FOOD STYLIST	Abby Stolfo
FOOD STYLIST	Alicia Deal
ILLUSTRATORS	Michael Schwab, Carolyn Gibb

ACKNOWLEDGEMENTS

Weldon Owen wishes to thank the following people for their generous support in producing this book: Lesley Bruynesteyn, Penny Flood, Derek Fong, Alexey Gulenko, Amy Hatwig, Becca Martin, Carolyn Miller, Sharon Silva, Jane Tunks, Emely Vertiz, Elysa Weitala, Xi Zhu

ADDITIONAL PHOTO CREDITS

Elise Bauer of SimplyRecipes.com: pages 40-41; Giada Canu/Stocksy: page 47; Maren Caruso: page 84; Andrew Cebulka/Stocksy: page 37; Monica Etcheverry/Getty Images: pages 168-169; Mee Productions/Stocksy: page 237; Tarbell Studio Photo/Shutterstock: endpapers; Jessica Theroux: author photo

ILLUSTRATION CREDITS

Michael Schwab: La Vie Rustic rooster logo, pages 11-12, 135-136; Carolyn Gibb: all other illustrations

Library of congress cataloging
in publication data is available.

ISBN-13 978-1-68188-143-0
ISBN-10: 1-68188-143-8

10 9 8 7 6 5 4 3 2 1
2016 2017 2018 2019

Printed and bound in China